CLUES
W9-CBC-203

IN SEARCH OF HERESY

BOOKS BY JOHN W. ALDRIDGE

After the Lost Generation
Critiques and Essays on Modern Fiction, 1920–1951 (Editor)
In Search of Heresy

IN SEARCH OF HERESY

American Literature in an Age of Conformity

by JOHN W. ALDRIDGE

KENNIKAT PRESS, INC./PORT WASHINGTON, N. Y.

IN SEARCH OF HERESY

Reissued in 1967 by Kennikat Press by arrangement

Library of Congress Catalog Card No: 67-16254

Manufactured in the United States of America

For my wife Leslie

ACKNOWLEDGMENTS

A MAJOR PORTION of the material of this book was first presented in the form of lectures delivered in the Christian Gauss Seminars in Criticism at Princeton University during the spring of 1954. Some of the same material, along with much of the remainder, later appeared in *The Nation, The New Leader, The New York Times Book Review, Virginia Quarterly Review,* and *Mandrake,* to the editors of which I am grateful for reprint permission. I wish to acknowledge special indebtedness to the members of the Seminars Committee at Princeton, particularly to E. B. O. Borgerhoff and R. P. Blackmur, for enabling me to undertake the work which made this book possible, and to them as well as to V. S. Pritchett, Sean O'Faolain, Alfred Alvarez, R. W. B. Lewis, and the other Seminars participants for creating an atmosphere of close critical attentiveness from which I gained stimulus, encouragement, and far more corrective instruction than I was able to put to use. My thanks are due also to the great editor and friend who suggested the title for this book. I owe, finally, a debt too personal for public definition to Mr. and Mrs. Samuel Blatt, and another equally great to my wife Leslie Felker Aldridge, whose warm devotion and moral courage have immeasurably enriched the isolation imposed by the writing of the book as well as that other, perhaps more permanent isolation which heresy imposes upon itself.

I should like to extend special thanks to the periodicals *New World Writing, Partisan Review,* and *The Paris Review* for permission to quote from the articles by Charles Fenton, Donald Hall, Allen Tate, Lionel Trilling, Delmore Schwartz, and William Styron. I want finally to thank the publishers for permission to quote from the following books: The Viking Press, Inc., for *The Adventures of Augie March,* by Saul Bellow, and for *The Liberal Imagination,* by Lionel Trilling; Albert and Charles Boni, Inc., for *Some Do Not,* by Ford Madox Ford; Houghton Mifflin Company for *The Heart Is a Lonely Hunter,* by Carson McCullers; The Bobbs-Merrill Company, Inc., for *Lie Down in Darkness,* by William Styron; Yale University Press for *Psychology and Religion,* by Carl Jung; Charles Scribner's Sons for *The Sun Also Rises,* by Ernest Hemingway.

J. W. A.

CONTENTS

IN SEARCH OF HERESY

INTRODUCTION

The choice of heresy

THE GREEK ETYMON of heresy is *haíresis,* which means a taking or choice. In English the word has come to mean an opinion or doctrine at variance with the orthodox or accepted. I suppose we do not need to speculate very long over the point that what for the ancient world carried the connotation of choice, the application of will to morals, has become for us a violation of law, incriminating will and morals alike. That is simply apt to happen in history when will loses supremacy as an instrument of moral choice: law replaces will; legality replaces choice; both replace morals. But it is true that we think in and act from symbols of language, and perhaps equally true that a symbol dies out in language when the act it symbolizes dies out in life. If heresy has lost the older connotation of choice, it may well be because the possibility of heresy as choice has receded from us. At any rate, I assume—and it is the assumption underlying most of the essays in this book—that some such recession has taken place and that we have suffered the effects in nearly all the areas in which some purpose beyond that of blind survival is required for the successful conduct of life.

I do not know how to make this real to those who have not already discovered it for themselves or who prefer to remain oblivious of what they have discovered, but it is a fact of habitual daily apprehension for some, and examples of its reality abound. Alfred North Whitehead gave one of the simplest illustrations when he observed that the modern housewife, unable to buy cloth in a particular shade of blue and obliged to content herself with whatever shade happens to be mass-produced, is experiencing at the most immediate level the effects both of enforced democratization of taste and of infringement upon the democratic right of free choice, the two together constituting one of the deranging paradoxes of life in the modern world. The point is that the housewife cannot commit a heresy in either sense of the word no matter how desperately she wants to, for the means are simply not available. In time, of course, she ceases to want to, for the urge toward heresy, like taste, atrophies unless allowed exercise: she forgets her shade of blue along with her reasons for preferring it to all other shades, and begins to like the shade she has no choice but to take. In loftier and more rigorous pursuits we are all similarly diminished for lack of some special shade of blue, and with an equally compromising effect upon our powers of choice. It is the risk we are forever running as mass men in a mass culture; it is the risk we can least afford to run as human beings.

In a certain narrow sense, the political history of our epoch may be read as a study in the decline of choice-making ideological positions. What feudalism provided was a closed system of immutable choices; it left behind a predatory freedom hard bent on the search for limits within which its energies could be confined and put to work, within which choice could once again become possible on a scale of clear alternatives. The various forms which modern politics has taken—fascism, communism, monarchy, liberal democracy—supplied for a time both limits and scale; they represented at once crystallizations of choice and positions from which choice could be made and action taken, for they functioned to simplify and organize reality and to bring it within the compass of the mass mind and under the control of the mass will. Ultimately, of course, most of these positions hardened into dogma or they died out, and when that happened, those that survived as dogma ceased to be choice-making positions and became positions from which the choosing had all long since been done. In this form they could either enforce orthodoxy or foment heresy (in the newer sense of the word), stabilize themselves or give way to an altered version of themselves, but once stabilized they could no longer support choice because the alternatives necessary to choice had been canceled out by dogma.

At the present time we have limited and largely ceremonial monarchy, dogmatic Soviet socialism (which is one of the heresies of dogmatic theoretical communism), denationalized and, for the most part, disarmed fascism, and conformist capitalistic democracy (which is one of the heresies of liberal capitalistic democracy). Of these perhaps Soviet socialism alone has remained in force as both dogma and ideological position.

American democracy can scarcely be said any longer to constitute a dogma (a fact which has crippled our best efforts to propagandize it abroad), nor can its conformism be called an ideological position (a fact which has not at all crippled the worst efforts of some of us to confer upon it the dignity of one). It is a feature of our democracy that it has no dogma to enforce, but neither does it enforce its conformism. It does not need to because it produces conformism by leaving open to the mass of people no alternative to conformism and, therefore, by removing from them the possibility of choice. This, I suspect, is at the heart of that paralysis of will, that derangement of the sense of future, which appears to be so prevalent today, especially among younger Americans. Our democracy in its current form gives them neither a dogma which might provide a basis for heretical action nor an opportunity to discover and choose a politics or faith or way of life which would represent a heresy of democracy. That is simply the certain shade of blue which our political mass-production does not supply. But our present way of life does supply conformity, conformity to the institutional, the corporate, and the civic interests, and so the young people conform in ever increasing numbers, forgetting their certain shade of blue and their reasons for wanting it, learning to want what there is to get.

In the case of the American intellectual, this condition asserts itself as a threat to morale and action alike, for it has traditionally been the intellectual's task—assigned and condoned by no one but himself—to monitor the culture of his time, to exercise within it his right of free choice, and upon it the reprimanding influence of his dissent. But standing between him and the performance of this task today are certain obstacles sufficiently distinct from those facing the culture in general as to be called peculiarly his own. The American intellectual has first of all suffered the loss in recent years of the older sustaining ideologies and platforms of dissent: he became disaffected long ago with the revolutionary ideal of communism, which afforded him an angle of critical vision into politics during the thirties, and he has outgrown the naïveté which once enabled him to shout down on the head of American materialism from one of the posts of romantic disaffiliation like that of the Artist in Exile. One can in fact say that he has been uprooted or evicted from just about all the positions which formerly justified and ennobled the isolation of his role and which held out some respectable alternative to the state of being merely cooperative and pleasant required by mass society. The result has been that the intellectual, deprived of alternative, has grown increasingly vulnerable to the enticements of conformism, for while it is true that conformism at the present time is neither dogmatic nor enforced, it does have interests in the service of which the talents of the intellectual may be profitably put to use, and rewards to which his past innocence of reward renders him peculiarly susceptible. But above all, conformism has on its side the fact, perhaps more compelling for the intellectual than for the average citizen, that as a platform for action it is all there is: the margin of possibility for action beyond conformism has been cut down to nothing. The paternalism of the cultural institutions, the institutional values of money, status, security, and power, have filled and padded the vacuum left by the loss of the values of disaffiliation and dissent.

The absence of an active alternative to conformism is attested to not only by the emptiness of some of the recent novels of dissent but by certain others which affirm conformism the most strongly. One of the most popular of these, Herman Wouk's *Marjorie Morningstar,* never dramatizes the heresy of which the conformist values it insists upon are the dogma. Although Marjorie is attracted briefly by the "nonconformity" of Noel Airman, it soon becomes clear that this is merely an adolescent posture of Noel's and has behind it neither ideological conviction nor a vision of any way of life which can incorporate it. Similarly, the American intellectual is handicapped for lack of a nonconformist program of action. Both his professional function and his way of life are necessarily carried on within a convention impossible to distinguish from that of his conformist neighbor. In a society such as the one Sinclair Lewis satirized —an earlier phase of our own—in which conformism is based on strongly held ideas of respectability, personal honor, success, and civic virtue, which assert themselves in prudery, philistinism, and hatred of culture, an alternative is of course easy to conceive: a way of life incorporating simply the opposites of these values. But present-day conformism is not morally or ethically based, but rather emphasizes passive and amoral qualities—comfort, security, peace of mind—which do not represent a dogma nor suggest a heresy. (For further discussion of conformism in fiction see Author's Note, Essay Four.)

The essays in this book were written for a variety of different occasions and are not intended to constitute a formal or systematic inquiry into the conformist tendencies now dominant in the American intellectual life. If they had been so intended, I should have included with them a great deal of related material not here included. Yet each of the major essays has to do with aspects of the conformist development. In them, at times singly, at times variously, I have been concerned with such matters as the new liberal assent to mass cultural values (particularly the new egalitarian frenzy which may be observed among certain intellectuals who formerly prided themselves on their minority status, when such status was still serviceable), the movement of literary intellectuals into the universities, and their adoption of the values of institutional orthodoxy, and the dramatic possibilities which appear to be open to the novelist in the conformist culture of the present time. Much of the remaining material represents an effort, which I hope will be taken as tentative and exploratory, to define a relation between this problem of a culture's dramatic potential—deriving from the concerns which it deems to be morally valuable—and the kind and quality of fiction a culture produces. Essays Three, Four, and Five, in particular, may be read as a single unit of discussion centering in this problem. But lest I be accused of advocating under the guise of an attack on conformism a return to some of the orthodoxies of the past, I had perhaps better make it clear that I am concerned in these essays with the kind of orthodoxy which, because it is backed by morals, religious principles, and social codes of manners, helps to make possible the delineation of scene and character in fiction. I do not say that such an orthodoxy is right or wrong in any sense except the esthetic, for I do suggest that it undoubtedly serves the novelist better than a situation of conformism which is not morally or religiously motivated and is, therefore, likely to be less dramatizable.

The point of view from which I approach the new intellectual conformism rests on an ideal which—as I have already suggested—is now anachronistic, unworkable, and quite without adherents, except for a few mavericks like myself who have not yet learned to reconcile the contrary teachings of their heads and hearts. I mean the ideal of creative independence and free critical dissent which has come down to us in the central tradition of American thought and letters and which has energized the work, even as it has debilitated more than a few of the lives, of most of the writers whom we now consider to be important. Cooper, Emerson, Melville, Hawthorne, Twain, Whitman, Crane, Norris, Dreiser, Mencken, Faulkner, and Hemingway have all adhered to it in their several ways. Yet even in them one can see that it was never pure, that it always existed side by side with its opposite in a moral nesting of impeding ambiguity. For it is clear that they wished to be accepted by the institutions they attacked, by the society to which they could not conform, that they longed to be loved by those they hated and condemned, and, above all, that they expected to be honored *for* their hatred and condemnation. But this has always been the figure in the carpet of American literature, the recurring case with writers both American and foreign, and it is the case again with this book: its dissent is assent inverted; it contains and affirms the dogma of which it is a heresy.

If this is a paradox, I suspect we had better embrace it, for it may well represent our certain shade of blue, what is left to us of the possibility of heresy as choice. For clearly the old easy positions and solutions will no longer suffice. We will perhaps do best to choose and submit to complexity and difficulty, contradiction, paradox, and failure, to insist again and again on the duty of the writer to be free, even as the range of his freedom grows daily narrower and his grasp on its meaning and use daily more tenuous, to assert the need to oppose conformism even though the culture presents no alternative to it, nor even a defensible "position" from which it can be opposed—to learn, in short, what another romantic once said it was possible only for the best of us to learn: how to hold two opposing ideas in the mind at the same time and still retain the ability to function. For it appears to be our fate, as it has been the fate of our literature as a whole, to have to hold together, without hope of resolution, the forces of dogma and heresy, conformity and dissent, hate and love, guilt and innocence, sin and redemption, and to create out of the holding itself the tension which brings art to life and life alive in art. What James's Dencombe saw as the truth of his own condition we have no choice now but to see as ours: "We work in the dark—we do what we can—we give what we have. Our doubt is our passion, and our passion is our task."

ONE

The situation of the American writer *

THOSE OF US who are now thirty or slightly older have already outlived the literary movement in which we grew up—the movement that came to fruition in the twenties, while we were still too young to participate in it, but that seemed destined for a time in the late forties to be given new vitality and purpose by writers our own age who were then coming out of the war. The great early figures of that movement—Yeats, Joyce, Gide, Shaw, Eliot, Pound—are nearly all dead now, their works and effects abandoned to the museums and the damp hands of classical scholarship. Later figures of the second rank like Scott Fitzgerald and Thomas Wolfe, whom we thought

* This essay was originally presented as a Christian Gauss lecture at Princeton under the title, "Thoughts on *Never* Being Bibliographed." The reference is to Edmund Wilson's famous essay. By echoing his style and tone in treating material very similar to his, I hoped to emphasize both the parallels and the ironic differences between the historical occasions of his essay and mine.

of, ten or fifteen years ago in college, as older but still active contemporaries of ours, have already taken on the remote character of minor deities out of some vanished Augustan past. Of the best writers now in middle age and still capable of serious work, only a very few have been able to develop at all significantly those initial and, for the most part, narrow insights into modern life which secured their place in the literary world of twenty years ago. The one or two—I can think of only Faulkner and Hemingway—whose later careers have been something more than a falling off or merely a repetition of earlier promise are chronically under siege by hordes of critics bent on sacking their establishments, picking over their bones, and raising around their works sepulchers of exegesis and bibliography. Some of the lesser known and, one would suppose, more fortunate writers of the same age—the one-book novelists and former poets—who sank into obscurity right after the twenties and for years were not heard of again, have suddenly been rediscovered and crowned with the notoriety of Civil War veterans and Titanic survivors for having once belonged to the movement or figured in the memoirs of someone who did.

The situation of the younger group of novelists is far different today from what it was seven or eight years ago when they first began to appear. At the time a variety of circumstances seemed to be coming together to produce an atmosphere both exciting and liberating to new talent. The war had ended without that fatigued suspension of the will which followed after 1918 and gave rise to the earlier literature of nervelessness; and there had finally come a break—sometime in the early forties—in the tendency of the proletarian school to repeat itself endlessly in novels rank with the outmoded economics of Marx and Engels. The reading public, which, while the war lasted, had been more or less content to subsist on the sweetnesses of Private Hargrove and William Saroyan, was now anxious for a return to the sterner realities; and publishers were finding it profitable to cultivate writers who, fresh from the hardships of active service, seemed most likely to bring it about. There began a rather grandiose and indiscriminate exploitation of every literary effect, good or bad, in any way connected with the war, of every young man with a combat trauma or gripe that could be turned to print.

Twenty-five and thirty years earlier this kind of wholesale speculation in talent had been a natural response to the upsurge of creative activity which came on in the twenties and which quickly began to be exploited with the competitive zeal normally associated with bull-market buying in Wall Street. Publishers gambled on dozens of young writers in the hope of discovering a new Sherwood Anderson or Sinclair Lewis, and ended, in certain historic instances, by discovering Ernest Hemingway, Scott Fitzgerald, and John Dos Passos, whose successes over the years that followed were in large part responsible for the rise of the great serious reputations of such houses as Scribner's and Houghton Mifflin. But now, at the end of another war, with the precedent of early subsidy of talent thus established and vindicated, what had formerly been speculative became self-conscious, and there grew up a feeling that literary renaissance and boom were known chemical compounds that could be precipitated into being if only one followed the formula of the past and paid enough money.

For the enterprising publisher of the forties this meant a

mechanical repetition of all the old conjuring tricks. Once again he bought up his stable of fresh young talent, although this time in the hope of discovering a new Hemingway, Fitzgerald, or Dos Passos; and it was not surprising that most of the writers he bought were those who, by an odd process of commercialized reincarnation, most closely resembled the masters whom he hoped to replace. Nor was it any more than inevitable that the ceremonies of first publication for many of these writers should seem to be patterned increasingly after those ancient rites of fertility in which the effigy of the dead god—or in this case the dead reputation—was cast into Hades to be born anew in the person of youth. After a while it became hard to avoid wondering whether the process of authorship was not really becoming one of ghoulish collaboration with the dead and dying, whether the first novel of Merle Miller or Robert Lowry was not in fact a new revision of *Tender Is the Night* done by Theodore Dreiser with the help of Compton McKenzie.

Yet in spite of the extremes of mercantile silliness to which it was occasionally carried, the quasi renaissance of the late forties had for a time an effect both exhilarating and wholesome on the younger writers themselves. It gave them enough money so that they were freed, very early in their careers, from the pressures of other work; and now that the war had ended, along with the restrictions which it had imposed on movement, it suddenly became possible with money to live the literary life once again, to throw big parties, to travel and settle abroad, to found magazines, with an ease and directness unknown since the twenties. It was in fact one of the most ironic features of the time that the commercial interests which had generated and then exploited the prevailing atmosphere of assiduous trendmongering and ancestor worship had also inadvertently brought about a condition in which both the more serious and the more frivolous interests of the past could actually for the first time in years be restored and developed. The financial collapse of the thirties had led to a shrinkage of nearly all the values of the intellectual life and had reduced writers from their former high position as free producers to the status of charity cases and wards of a welfare state. Their Marxist concerns, moreover, had had the effect of temporarily anesthetizing their sense of any purpose for art beyond that of social relevance, just as, in the early forties, the official wartime view of their "responsibility," huckstered by such new patriots as Archibald MacLeish and Bernard De Voto, had persuaded some of them to desert politics for propaganda.

But now, for those of the younger group who continued to be benefited rather than stifled or debauched by the constant iteration of the names and works of famous predecessors, the flattering juxtaposition of earlier creative decades with their own, there was set up a frame of mind and reference in which it became natural once again to speak of a serious disinterested calling of American letters and of a native tradition of excellence on which the beginning writer could take his bearings. The promising young novelist with his first book completed enjoyed not merely the customary guaranty of publication provided him by the boom but the greater advantage of feeling himself launched into history and placed almost at once in an established line of influence which perhaps he was simultaneously appointed to carry on. While it was not always obvious to him that his eminence had been concocted or that, more often than not, he was being made simply the pawn of a publicity enterprise bent on exploiting the exchange value of the past, he was nevertheless given a sense of belonging, however tentatively, to a traditional hierarchy of peers to whom the practice of literature was a common craft and faith in its importance a common motivation.

In any case, by the end of the forties the opening phase of the postwar literary revival had run its course, publishing had settled down to a state of seemingly permanent inflation, and conditions became different again. The younger novelists who, three or four years previously, had written their first books in a spirit of confidence that they were entering on a new creative cycle and carrying forward an established creative tradition suddenly found themselves high and dry in a world where all they stood for seemed to have gone into eclipse and where they themselves had become premature anachronisms. Although they had, as a group, by now published a respectable body of work, including several novels of genuine distinction, and had among them such accomplished writers as Jean Stafford, Carson McCullers, John Horne Burns, Norman Mailer, Paul Bowles, and Truman Capote, they had largely failed to take the positions of authority and influence which had appeared to be opening to them only a short time before. In fact, the situation with which they were now confronted was such as to invalidate entirely the system of accession to power and prominence, the very possibility of reputation in the old sense, which had been the feature of the decades just past and on which, in the excitement of the immediate postwar years, they had come to pin their hopes. The modern literary movement had, in those years, lost nearly all its potency as a reproductive and energizing force and had been slowly absorbed into the universities, where its massive indignations had cooled down to small fastidious tics experienced by graduate students in the damp undercaves of libraries, and where its great seminal ideas * had been frozen and crystallized into churchly authoritarian dogma. The leaders and apostles of the movement whom the younger group had thought of as their natural and at least spiritually living mentors appeared now to have been embalmed and mummified like ancient Egyptian priests and set up in niches to commemorate the grandeur of a vanished cult, while their works had come to be looked upon, not as models to be admired and imitated but as sacred canonical treasures to be studied as objects of research in the science of liturgics. Literature now was a corporate body, official, institutionalized, and closed: the appearance of a new writer, the creation of a new work outside the canon was not only irrelevant but irreverent, at best a willful and rather nasty breach of etiquette, at worst very nearly an act of heresy. Besides, the consolidation of literary

* It would undoubtedly be fatuous to attempt any categorical definition of these ideas. They cannot merely be listed, for that is to burlesque history and insult intelligence. Nor can they be purposefully discussed as if they enjoyed some spectacular distinction not to be found in ideas underlying the literary movements of other cultures and ages. But I do have in mind the special emphasis given in this century and the last to certain ageless assumptions about the nature of literature and the role of the writer in society. One cannot begin to distinguish the movement I speak of from others without taking this emphasis into account, particularly as it shows itself in the metaphysical-symbolist influence in poetry, the realist-symbolist influence in fiction, and the formalist influence in criticism, this is to say, in the line of literary development carried forward in modern times by Rimbaud, Baudelaire, and Flaubert and by Conrad, James, Joyce, Richards, and Eliot. If the modern movement can be said to have a bias, it is in the direction of the impressionist outgrowth of Romanticism. That, at any rate, is the feature which our best criticism has recognized as the badge of artistic seriousness and worth.

power within the universities had progressed to the point where the manufacture of new writers and works could be carried out under the controlled conditions of the laboratory and the tested and purified techniques of the masters injected like plasma directly into the blood streams of apprentices, enabling them to begin at once to write poems rich in ambiguity, paradox, irony, symbolism, and tension, and short stories and novels incorporating James's device of the "trapped spectator," Conrad's concealed and multiple narrators, and Joyce's parallels to the myth of Odysseus.

There was something suspect and vulgar now about a writer who worked up his own materials or who retained more than a speculative interest in the experience of his own time. To the literary men of the academy he seemed to inhabit some distastefully fetid underworld of subintellectual intrigue, a kind of retarded bohemian cellar, where the cold, clear light of Brooks and Warren never penetrated. But the independent writer had what was, from the academic point of view, the still more crippling defect of being unable or unwilling to keep abreast of the current developments in his field. He thought of himself, for example, as belonging to the avant-garde and as carrying forward a tradition of free creative inquiry into the spirit of his age; while the truth was that his entire conception of the avant-garde—the conception of a community of intransigent, revolutionary talents—had long since been outmoded by the rise of a new academic avant-garde conceived in the name of orthodoxy and dedicated to the principle that all writers are created equal provided they conform to the rules of the canon. As for the work of free creative inquiry into the spirit of the age, it had been purged both of freedom and of creativeness and entrusted to a special commission headquartered in the *Partisan Review,* where it became known henceforward simply as "Project X: *explication du Zeitgeist.*"

The movement, finally, to which the independent writer naïvely felt himself to be still allied had not merely become institutionalized in the universities; it had passed into the receivership of the new avant-garde and been turned into capital for an official corporation of "experimental" literature, presided over by a board of director-critics, staffed by graduates of the literary workshops at Stanford and Iowa, and headquartered in the *Kenyon* and *Sewanee Reviews.* Here the process of direct exploitation of the masters of the movement —which had begun in the universities with the creation of synthetic, junior-sized Joyces, Jameses, and Kafkas—was accelerated to the point where it passed into the large-scale production of hybrid and mutated forms of those special dramatic techniques which criticism had explicated out of the works of the masters. Thus, instead of reading James, the young avant-gardist read Percy Lubbock on *The Ambassadors* and made use in his novel of Lubbock's interpretation of James's use of "point of view"; instead of reading Faulkner, he read Richard Chase on the images of line and curve in *Light in August* and began distributing through his novel, at the rate of about three to the page (that being the "holy" number), images of line and curve. He discovered in time, of course, that for the successful employment of these techniques some subjects served better than others: some would symbolize, others would not; some met the official specifications as to "resonance, thickness, and depth," others were dangerously experiential and naturalistic and threatened to trap him into a single level of meaning or a failure to render or evoke.

There consequently grew up a special avant-garde etiquette of subject selection which became as restrictive in its effects on the quarterlies as the clichés and stereotypes imposed by the mass audience on the commercial magazines. A primary requirement was that a short story be presented against a background of sufficient complexity and dimension to make possible the objectification of theme through the natural elements of landscape and weather—a device made mandatory after the Robert W. Stallman researches into the work of Stephen Crane and Conrad. The best stories, therefore, were those set in such locales as the wild mountain country of the West and the decadent bayou and hill country of the South, where the majestic or baroque furnishings of environment could be made to serve as correlatives for the emotional responses of character. The situations themselves which could be expected to rise out of of these locales were naturally limited in kind. They tended to turn on the mechanism of the muffled psycho-religious epiphany—the canonical equivalent of Aristotle's recognition-reversal sequence—and to have to do with adolescent hayloft intrigues, the death of small pet animals on Montana ranches, the sadism of sinisterly precocious Mississippi children, the menopausal sex adventures of middle-aged gentlewomen with faithful old plantation retainers, and the sensibility crises of lonely young girls in Virginia boarding schools. Stories of this type appeared to result from the writers' calculated effort to make use of materials which were conceived by the academy to be "literary"—because rustic or bizarre—

and to have been drawn out of what few timid sorties into "felt life" they themselves had had the opportunity to launch prior to their matriculations in the workshops and graduate schools.

As their memory of life faded, however, along with their capacity to feel it, many of them began exploiting the world of the academy itself; and there set in among them a species of creative incest in which the relations which normally obtain between writers and their experience were perverted into relations with the agency which instructed or supported them in the art of having relations with their experience. The prototypal result was the work of "in-group" exposé, the academic *conte* and *roman à clef* such as Mary McCarthy's *The Groves of Academe* and Randall Jarrell's *Pictures from an Institution,* in which the dramatic interest centered neither in the "felt life" nor in the quality of the rendered emotion—of which there was usually none—but in the verisimilitude with which known institutions and personages were represented and satirized. And as these became in time increasingly easy to identify, it began to be evident that there existed even a formal avant-garde etiquette for scandal, a conventionalized snobbery which limited the area of satirical attack to certain selected institutions and personages—notably, to Bennington, Bard, and Sarah Lawrence colleges, their faculties and presidents—and which ruled out places like Columbia and the universities of Chicago, Michigan, and Wisconsin as presumably fit for investigation only in novels of a low naturalistic order or of merely reformist intent.

By the same token, the avant-garde writers themselves existed within carefully restricted lines of status and class.

In issue after issue of the quarterlies one read the same names at the heads of stories—Randall Jarrell, Mary McCarthy, Walter Van Tilburg Clark, Eudora Welty, Saul Bellow, Elizabeth Hardwick, Flannery O'Connor, Jean Stafford, Shirley Jackson, Katherine Anne Porter, Robie Macauley—and when the quarterly reviewers devoted their characteristically scrupulous attention to fiction at all, it was almost certainly to be to the work of these same writers. Those, on the other hand, who like Norman Mailer, Calder Willingham, James Jones, John Horne Burns, Irwin Shaw, Alfred Hayes, Gore Vidal, and Chandler Brossard, had come up outside the universities and had, for better or worse, remained free of affiliation except to their craft, were just as scrupulously ignored. They were apparently thought of as too unrestrainedly creative and, therefore, by an odd but typical logic, as insufficiently literary and serious. Their novels had to do with such subjects as war, race prejudice, sexual aberration, social maladjustment, neurosis, and insanity, or simply the way it was in 1945 or the winter of 1947, and these—now that the academy had attended to the burial of both the older realism and naturalism—were considered outside the province of the novel and suitable only as raw materials for sociologists, psychiatrists, and other case workers in merely human experience.

Besides, the novel now was a classic form; it had evolved beyond the point where it could be used easily, exploratively, or imperfectly, with any hope of adapting it to the conditions of new work. All one could legally do was produce small, mathematically perfect scale models of an institutionalized abstraction known simply as "novel," and then one had to be careful, for even in effigy the novel had at least to wear the look of a strained and suffocating greatness. It consequently came about that the majority of these younger writers, although they represented the only really fresh and independently creative element to appear in the postwar generation, found themselves cut off, at the outset of their careers, from both the established avant-garde and the centers of the one respectable critical authority to which they might have looked for guidance, understanding, and the means of serious reputation.

Meanwhile, in the literary market place a parallel situation was beginning to emerge. The publishing boom, which had been steadily gaining momentum through the five years following the war, had reached proportions by 1950 so fantastically beyond the power of any human agency to imagine or control that one supposed the manufacture of books to have been taken over in the night by some monstrous, self-operating, perpetual-motion machine diabolically bent on conquering the world by smothering its inhabitants beneath tons of print. One was encouraged in this impression by the spectacle of the publishers themselves, many of whom appeared to have been converted into the captive host-creatures of an autotelic business enterprise whose original purposes had been lost in antiquity and whose sole remaining function was simply to keep on endlessly and pointlessly running.

It seemed suddenly that all the old categories and relationships which had formerly guided and comforted one in one's thinking about the production of books had gone into the discard or had, like so many of one's old assumptions, simply ceased after the war to correspond to reality—if, indeed, there can be said to have been a reality after the war. It scarcely mattered, for example, that books had at one time been the results of the painful and loving efforts of intelligent men to communicate something which they conceived to be worthwhile, that they had been meant to *say* something, and by their saying to satisfy a very real and existing human need. Books now were simply disposable items containing a two- or three-hour supply of psychic maintenance; when they were used up, they could be thrown away like Kleenex. There was no longer any question of their satisfying a need, nor was it necessary any longer that they should. For a public accustomed from childhood to buying at the dictates of every passing acquisitive reflex, it was enough that books were offered on the market for sale, that they were simply *there* to be bought. They would undoubtedly still have been bought in large numbers if they had been nothing but bundles of blank paper sewn into gaudy covers.

In the midst of all this the writers of the younger group who had begun their careers during the first phase of the boom were caught up in conditions so radically different from those which prevailed at that time that it is no wonder many of them lost their bearings and, in some cases, after remarkable initial successes lapsed into silence or mediocrity. The rise of mass publishing had effectively brought to an end the period of innovation and discovery into which they emerged, and where they had formerly been made to feel special and chosen by virtue of being young writers upon whom the accolade of posterity was about to be bestowed, they now found themselves regarded simply as slightly older members of a transient, anonymous body of writers all of whom seemed equally young, equally talented, and equally forgettable. Not only had the traditional public image of the writer as a figure of glamour apparently faded along with the decline of interest in books, but there had grown up a widespread indifference to the fact of talent itself, and a feeling that fiction of whatever quality somehow no longer communicated any vision of reality which it was possible to respond to or recognize as true. Although novels of distinction were still being written, one could scarcely imagine a way in which they might have been received with even approximately the kind of immediate shock of recognition that accompanied the appearance of novels like *The Great Gatsby* and *The Sun Also Rises,* nor did there seem any possibility of their being preserved in the public consciousness long enough to be revived in ten or twenty years and accorded a similar place in the hierarchy of modern classical literature. The truth now was statistical and political; it yielded to the forces of tabulation and analysis, the devices of the survey, the corporate report, the personal interview and the house-to-house poll, rather than to imaginative synthesis. The works of Dr. Kinsey, C. Wright Mills, David Riesman, Susanne K. Langer, and other sociophilosophical thinkers were the substitutes for major fiction in the fifties and made use of insights into contemporary culture which would undoubtedly in any other time have found their most natural expression in the novel form.

There was, furthermore, a sense in which it could be said that publishing had by now evolved to the point where its business interests were no longer best served by the novelist of quality but by the second- or third-rate writer who could be counted on to turn out in large volume and at fast pace a kind of pseudo fiction, a species of high-grade, extremely serious hack writing—of which Herman Wouk's *The Caine*

Mutiny is one example—containing all the ingredients of the real thing but in diluted or homogenized form, so that it could be fed over and over again to readers without ever bringing them to the stage of satisfaction where they would cease to buy. Many of the first novels by the younger writers who were discovered in the early fifties belonged to this category—including a few, like John Phillip's *The Second Happiest Day*, which were singled out for special praise by critics on the ground of their "sincerity"—and that was perhaps one of the reasons for the falling off of interest in the younger literary generation as such. But as more and more novels of all kinds were published, each tended anyway, regardless of its quality, to be reduced in value to the level of all the others and treated in the same anonymous manner. And as the promotional agencies of publishing became increasingly petrified in their attitudes of soaring high encomium and the reviewing profession increasingly drugged on the volume of novels flooding into the market, there finally remained no method of distinguishing good from bad or of separating out the work most likely to be of more than passing interest.

In previous literary decades such as the twenties it had been possible—although one no longer knew quite how—for the novelist sooner or later to achieve a continuity of reputation and public success at least equal to the stamina and value of his work. One thought of the young Hemingway and the young Fitzgerald and of the inevitability of the process by which they rose, through regular stages of gradual growth and single successes, as well as instructive failures, to the positions of fame in which they finally became secure. But one also thought of those small centers of enthusiastic opinion—the magazines like the *Dial, Bookman, Hound and Horn,* the old *Saturday Review* and *New Republic,* and the columns and articles of men like Edmund Wilson, John Peale Bishop, Van Wyck Brooks, Stuart P. Sherman, and Burton Rascoe—where their names and books were not allowed to be forgotten, and of that initially small but receptive reading public which fancied that these writers were speaking to them and which in turn spoke back to them. One thought, in short, of the existence of certain sanctuaries where the memory of talent was preserved during the fallow time between the actual appearance of books. But now, in a time which seemed suddenly to have gone rotten with literature, the young writer of promise found himself in a situation in which he felt compelled perpetually to remake his public bed with each new work, until finally, in far too many cases, he became exhausted and was overcome with a desire just to lie down on the floor and go to sleep. With the appearance of each new book he was hustled forward to stand naked for a moment in the public gaze. He was extravagantly promoted and meanly or indifferently reviewed. For perhaps three weeks he was granted a sort of low-grade meretricious notoriety. But as soon as the reviews stopped coming in, he began to feel neglected, and in another month or so could consider himself lucky if an occasional literate reader remembered having seen his name.

Whatever his new book may have been, it stood small chance of being admitted to membership in a growing body of selected work which represented the accumulated literary achievement of his time. After the popular reviews had appeared, he did not, if he was typical, see his book discussed at length in the serious quarterlies, compared with the work of his contemporaries, or assigned a place in the larger critical order. There was no Ezra Pound or Ford Madox Ford to write him letters of encouragement and advice; he had little or no sense that what he had had to say had found an audience among those of his own age who had shared in his own experience. In a few months he was likely to be driven to conclude that his only hope for literary salvation lay in the quick production of another book, and then another and another and another, through which he might possibly gain by siege what he could not gain by honest stealth. But as the books came from him at increasingly shorter intervals, with each one perhaps bearing the increasingly unmistakable marks of technical haste and imaginative strain, he found himself going through the same old process, only now there were mounting reasons why he should slip backward two steps for every step forward he managed to take. In the end, he was likely to have discovered that in trying to build the public personality which his urge toward status demanded, he had drawn irrecoverably upon the creative capital which had been its sole justification and had succeeded only in cutting status from under his feet.

One has heard it argued—most recently with that hysteria of conviction which renders all conviction suspect—that the tremendous expansion of the paper-reprint industry during the boom years and the rise within the same medium of the mass-circulation literary review have done much to reduce, if not altogether to solve, the problems now confronting the serious writer. The large-scale manufacture of inexpensive reprints is said to have brought about in America a changed cultural situation in which the writer has been placed for the first time in contact with vast sectors of the average reading audience from which he had been formerly cut off; while the mass-circulation review has allegedly made it possible for him, again for the first time, to reach that audience with work of a new or an experimental kind which has hitherto been supposed unpalatable to it and, therefore, suited only to small-quarterly publication. It has been generally maintained that as a result of these developments the writer is now assured not only of the widest and most profitable market for his books but also of the chance to function up to his fullest capacity within that market without having to compromise his standards of artistic honesty and taste.

It is difficult to quarrel with these claims. One would prefer simply to accept them *in toto* as valid, for then one would be satisfied that the revolution for which, in one way or another, we have all so long been fighting had at last actually been won, and there would be nothing left to do but bury the ammunition, clear away the barricades, and settle down to work for the new coalition—as, in fact, many of our former colleagues of the underground have already been persuaded to do. But one is unfortunately still compelled to make distinctions, especially now in the face of a phenomenon which because of its enormous potentiality for good and the vastness of its implications for the future of our literature must always tend to appear to us in the shape of our wildest chimeras and to bedazzle us at every turn with the mirage of oasis. While it can hardly be denied that the rise to power of the reprint industry has profoundly altered the traditional relations between the writer and the mass audience as well as between the mass audience and the work of merit, it has yet to be proved that the lot of the writer has thereby, in a host of important respects, been appreciably bettered. There is much evidence for supposing, rather, that a number of partial and quasi satisfactions, backed by almost unbelievable financial returns, have been substituted for the real satisfactions which the writer has always needed to get from the circulation of his work but which appear to be farther from him now than ever before.

The abstract idea of mass audience has, for example, been allowed subtly to crowd out, by seeming to satisfy, the writer's constant need for a public. He has been handed sheaves of statistics indicating that the reprint sales of his books in the drugstores and on the newsstands have gone into the hundreds of thousands or millions, and he has complacently concluded that such figures represent the true magnitude of his readership and popularity. But what he does not know and cannot know, so long as the reprint system continues to operate on its present basis, is who his readers are and why they buy his books—whether they buy them because they are his or only because they just happened, while foraging among the racks, to come into titillating collision with their covers. By the same token, he does not know whether, if he publishes a reprint edition of another of his books, it will be bought by the same people who bought his last or will have to make its way with an entirely new set of readers.

And even if he is lucky enough to acquire readers specifically his own, the chances are that he will still come out the loser, for under the present distribution system, in which the wholesaler supplies his retail outlets in lot form rather than on the basis of individual orders for particular books, there is no way for readers to make their wants known or even to be certain that the works of their favorite author will ever again be available at a given outlet. The writer is thus placed in the most paradoxical of situations. Through the reprint market he gains access to an immense potential audience but never to an effective, articulate public. If his sales are at all typical, he achieves through that market the financial status of the established, successful writer but not the reputation, or the means of reputation, by which such status must be accompanied if it is ever to be real. He consequently finds himself with all his relations with his medium impoverished to the point where the only sense he has of his literary existence is that abstractly provided him by his sales reports and royalty checks.

The fallacy underlying the belief in the importance to the writer of an audience of sheer size is nowhere more clearly demonstrated than in the new mass-circulation reviews which have taken over the fallacy and inflated it into a first principle of editorial doctrine. Both *New World Writing* and *Discovery* —the two contenders in the field at the moment—have been represented by their sponsors as guaranteeing the writer all the freedoms that were available to him in the "little" magazines of the past along with the advantage of incomparably wider readership, hence, incomparably wider opportunities for acquiring reputation. Within the terms of the quantitative fallacy these claims are of course entirely valid; but once again one is compelled to make distinctions. The "little" magazines of the twenties and thirties came into being in response to the rise of a literary movement which was too revolutionary to win support in the existing commercial periodicals. Their audiences were always small, but they were vociferous and vocal, and they constituted the only kind of readership the serious writer ever really needs, a readership of peers and informed disciples through whom reputations can be initiated and preserved until such time as they are confirmed by the public at large.

New World Writing and *Discovery*, by rescuing the writer from what is conceived to be the obscurity of the small coterie public, have abandoned him to the infinitely more inpenetrable and permanent obscurity of the mass audience, where his influence is spread thin among thousands of inattentive minds and where his name is lost in the limbo of plenty. They have also placed him in circumstances which appear to have no purpose or objective, for it is characteristic of these reviews—as it is of so many of the products of our present drive to inflate still further by synthetic means the already bloated ego of literature—that they have no real cause to serve and no discernible demand to satisfy. They have grown up in response to no movement, and there is scarcely more than an academic sense in which it can be argued that they provide an outlet for work which would not have been acceptable—unless perhaps on grounds of quality—for publication elsewhere. They seem simply to have evolved out of a feeling that something approximating the "little" magazine probably ought to exist in our time and, by existing, might very well stimulate a movement or a fresh creative impulse to which it could then, albeit somewhat contrivedly, become a response. Such strained and self-conscious efforts to foment controversy as those recently made in *Discovery* by its editor, Vance Bourjaily, would lead one to believe this to be the case. But unfortunately, in choosing to make their way with the mass audience rather than with the coterie, these reviews have moved beyond the protection and support which the coterie alone can afford them and are brought up against a situation in which controversy can have no meaning or pertinence and in which new literature is simply used and discarded, without apparent motive or effect.*

* As the Age of the Paper Back continues, one fact becomes clear: the increase in volume of literary production has been accompanied by a decline in the possibility for development of any single literary reputation. This is especially true in the case of poetic reputations. In issue after issue of *New World Writing,* for example, the work of frequently talented new poets is introduced; yet one can already foresee a common doom for the talented and untalented alike. They are fated either to disappear or, perhaps worse, to go on endlessly and ineffectually appearing in *New World Writing,* gaining neither fame nor fortune. And this will be so because no one, certainly no constituted agency or body of readers, will ever single out for praise, quotation, or recollection this or that poem or line of theirs, and thus initiate around their names and work that slow accretion of interest which becomes reputation. It is a fact of no small concern that the names which dominate poetry at the present time—Eliot, Auden, Aiken, Williams, Thomas, Stevens—were all made famous by cultural circumstances of, at the very least, a decade ago, and that in our own decade we have no new comparably dominating name. We are being supported in poetry, in other words, as to a very large extent we are being supported in the novel, by men who were already masters when many of us were still in the grades. But we are by now familiar with the circumstances which made this odd situation possible—the shift of cultural interests which caused the modern literary movement first to be historicized, then institutionalized, then, most recently, democratized by those educational and critical agencies which sought to establish and indemnify a modern "movement" and which, in the case of poetry, derived much of their zeal from their worthy determination to educate the public out of its prejudice against the "difficulty" of modern poetic techniques. But whatever the causes, the shift occurred and the reputations were made. Today one cannot help but feel that the stock of the new poem or poet stands from the beginning at zero and is destined, barring a miracle, to remain at zero. It is not enough to suggest that the poet is perhaps not so good as Auden or Eliot. It is more to the point to admit that no one seems really to care enough to find out what he is. His work is presented with that of his fellows in such a magazine as *New World Writing,* and it at once becomes part of a "package," something to be read and discarded, but never used. The reader presumably tosses it aside with the feeling that he has "had" poetry for today, and that tomorrow or next week or next issue there will be other poetry and poets for him to "have." This is the final and most ghastly twist that can be given

It would be inaccurate to say that these conditions present themselves to the writer in the shape of a dilemma. That, in fact, precisely *is* his dilemma: that he does not and cannot know that he is in one. All the evils of his situation come to him wearing Yeats's mask of innocent virtue, and he has been so long accustomed to taking his satisfaction where he could find it—in the appearance of acclaim, the illusion of audience, the hypocrisy of status—that his need for the satisfaction to be gained from the real thing has atrophied and disappeared. In an earlier time one might have conceived this to be finally a question of integrity. But integrity implies the existence of a standard to be maintained, and its loss the existence of a temptation to which it can be sold. The irony and terror of the writer's dilemma today are that the question of his integrity can no longer be raised. In the name of what can he hold out? To which temptation does he have anything left to sell?

---

to Randall Jarrell's famous nightmare of the man who answered "Huh?" when asked if he ever read poetry. Today the man would answer "Yes."

TWO

The writer in the university

Now that the larger initiating impulses behind the modern cultural movement have died out, we are beginning to find ourselves confronted, as sooner or later we had to be, with various illusions and manufactures—what Tocqueville would have called "hypocrisies"—of cultural and literary situations. We are also beginning to find ourselves confronted, as sooner or later we deserved to be, with manufactures of cultural and literary men to inhabit and maintain these manufactures, men, this is to say, primarily dedicated not to the disinterested creation of cultural works—poems, paintings, novels, symphonies, plays—but to the exploitative use of the cultural institutions which have been raised around the act of creating these works. This, I take it, is what happens in a time when the creative impulse flags, becomes institutionalized, then dies out from under the institution, taking with it the satisfactions that formerly accrued from its use. The institution survives. But it survives solely as the public mode, the manufactured apparatus, of the creative impulse which launched it into being, and the satisfactions it provides become solely those which any and all institutions, cultural or otherwise, are able to provide—a little status, a little security, a little power—the hypocrisies of the original creative satisfactions.

The present cultural situation in America is everywhere alive with examples of this, of institutions which have lost their creative *raison* and have therefore substituted one or more of its various hypocrisies, bringing about that divorcement of action from impulse, existence from identity, emotion from response which is the feature of the castrating dualism of our time. The indisputable reality, to take one case, of that small but genuinely enlightened public on whose active response the artist could at one time count, and against whom he could define himself as real, has now been replaced—since it has ceased to be a reality—by a manufacture, a statistical construct, of a mass-consuming public whose existence is measured in numerals, the hypocrisy of audience, and whose capacity for response is computed in sales receipts, the hypocrisy of response. All the machinery of cultural production originally set up to satisfy the real demands of the initial small public has been gradually converted into an institutionalized apparatus designed to meet the largely hypothetical demands of the mass public. In the process, the popular arts have come more and more to resemble the canned and packaged goods obtainable at supermarkets: painters have taken to painting institutional abstractions of modernism, since modernism is no longer a movement or a creative mode but merely a fashion in window-dressing décor; writers have taken to turning out manufactures of novels, pretentious aphasia-inducing works with nothing in them but print, which the publishers nonetheless piously publish, the reviewers favorably review, and the public regularly buys—or just as regularly fails to buy—because the institutions of painting, writing, publishing, reviewing, buying, and nonbuying must all be kept going at whatever cost to reality, long after they have ceased to have any creative cause to serve.

All this is undoubtedly no more than the normal dirty politics of institutional survival. In the popular institutions it is perhaps of little importance, since there the amount of chicanery tends as a rule to vary inversely with the cultural value of the institution. But when one finds it becoming the habitual politics of mind for those who, as members of the intellectual classes, have the highest stake in the preservation of the serious values of the culture, it becomes a different matter altogether. I assume the institutionalization of the intellectual in America today to be an accomplished fact, his adoption of the hypocrisies of mass culture—conformism, assent to institutional values, distrust of creative values—to be the most unfortunate result of the process I have been describing. The attitudes of dissent and estrangement which the American intellectual formerly held toward the more exploitative aspects of his culture at least had the character of a deeply felt, genuinely emotive response. They were based not only upon a real dissatisfaction with real conditions in a real world but upon the promise held out by a socialist revolutionary ideal, the developing vitality of the modern cultural movement, and the continuing possibility of the free creative life. But with the corruption of this ideal, the decline of that vitality and freedom, the intellectual found himself in a position where it seemed he had no choice but to embrace all his former enemies, to accept for the real values in which he could no longer believe the manufactures of value which the culture could provide. And like most converts he became more assiduous in his faith than those to whom the faith was native. Because he could no longer love communism and the elite culture of Europe, he began to love democracy and the mass culture of America; and since anything less than total commitment was unthinkable to him, he felt obliged to love everything about America: equal rights, mass production, mass education, free enterprise, television, supermarkets, used cars, baseball games, Dr. Kinsey, President Eisenhower. He became with passion what he had formerly despised with reason. But as his testimonials of new faith and his confessions of old sins began to make clear, he could not honestly affirm with his emotions all the things which he had decided to affirm with his head. His protestations of love were poverty-stricken for objects worthy of love. His passion, like Eliot's version of Hamlet's hatred for his mother, was in excess of the real facts as they appeared, stronger than the capacity of the facts to call it forth, and so it lay on his conscience like a crime to muddle motive and stifle action—inexplicable, embarrassing, and suspect.

The formerly liberal journal *Partisan Review* has lately become the chief organ of the new intellectual orthodoxy. One is constantly being confronted in its pages by the spectacle of serious literary men, estranged from their former sources of creative value, frantically scurrying for cover beneath the skirts of the new American mother-symbol of mass egalitarian culture. Some of them, like Mr. Delmore Schwartz, have been driven by their urge toward womb immersion to the point where they have taken to issuing periodic self-immolating apologies in which they assert a pro-Americanism so extreme and calculated that it would make a native grass-roots fascist blush, and in which they claim ownership of more used cars, ranch-style houses, and television sets than the average citizen would find quite decent. Others have elevated the underlying metaphysics of this into a critical credo of even more sinister implications. One critic, for example, Mr. Leslie Fiedler, has devoted a large part of his recent book *An End to Innocence* to a detailed and at times extremely perceptive analysis of the major themes of American fiction, of which the dominant characteristic, running roughly from Cooper to James Jones, seems to him immaturity. In fact, it is I believe fair to say of Fiedler that he sees American fiction as one long documentary celebration of disguised adolescent homosexuality. Cooper's Chingachnook and Deerslayer, Melville's Ishmael and Queequeg, Twain's Huck and Jim, the poems of Whitman, the novels of Fitzgerald, the suspiciously comradely soldiers of Hemingway and Jones, the ambivalent little boy-girls and girl-boys of Capote and McCullers—all are to him cases in point. By the same token, both the American conception and the American practice of the literary life are cloyed, he feels, with immature romantic fantasies: the myth of the writer as a madman, dope fiend, drunkard, and bum; the naïve success dreams of a Fitzgerald; the burly-boy antics of a Hemingway; the sentimental cult of experience which drove so many good writers into European exile, there to squander their time and talents, or which paralyzed them in infantile attitudes of defiance and rebellion, the old postures for killing the father.

Over against this view of the American writer Fiedler sets the curative principle of maturity. He calls for a literary coming of age, a rise to full creative responsibility, which has precisely as healthy and right-minded a sound today as it had when Van Wyck Brooks first uttered it more than thirty years ago. But behind and beneath Fiedler's notion of maturity one soon senses a complex of assumptions, unconscious and otherwise, which are not so healthy and which seem right only if you adhere to a view of the right that negates both literature and maturity. Maturity, it becomes clear, is predicated for Fiedler upon the substantial figure of the urban orthodox man, the figure which throughout his book affords him his post of observation and judgment upon the American literary scene. The urban orthodox man is one who accepts calmly and detachedly his full share of social and moral responsibility: he is a good American, respectably married, a father, preferably of a large and happy family, a jobholder, a churchgoer, an active worker in community affairs, an owner of property; he may at the same time be an intellectual, for his society is nothing if not tolerant of small marginal differentiations, but he is not imaginative; he is certainly not so immature as to suppose himself a writer, although he may be a professor, a teacher of writing, or a part-time literary critic, one of the approved institutional forms of the writer. In short, against the childishly extravagant, socially disruptive values of the creative life Fiedler sets the orthodox values of the socially conformist life, values which appear to differ scarcely at all from those which the bourgeois mind has traditionally opposed to the creative. But this is not all; it is not nearly enough, for it throws too clean and innocuous a light upon the simple ambiguity of Fiedler's position. His orthodox man is no ordinary Babbitt. He is more precisely literature's twilight man, the artist *manqué* turned literary intellectual. He is what remains after a creative movement has spent itself, the lone Alexandrian fishing beside the dull canal, and he has that deathly wisdom that comes with missed opportunity and *fin de siècle*. He sees in his wisdom that creativity is, after all, a dead end, that literature is at best an aberration, that mostly only homosexuals and romantics who are not mature enough to acknowledge that they are homosexuals practice it, and that really the only recourse for the normal man, the mature man, is assent to the orthodoxies of mass society. In an odd way he is himself a romantic, precisely as much of a romantic as those whom he condemns, but he is disillusioned. Deep down in his heart he hates himself for not being a writer, and he hates literature for having somehow got on without him. So he rationalizes the position he cannot help but take: he destroys literature by finding it homosexual and thus unworthy of his devotion; he exhorts writers to put aside their childish nonsense, to grow up, stop trying to kill the father, settle down and marry with the mother, so that there will be no more writers around to give him guilt feelings. By means of these subterfuges he purges himself of his literary obligations and is freed to affirm the various hypocrisies of creative satisfactions that are left to him to affirm—the institutions of the home, family, religion, community, the American way, and the *status quo*.

This affirmation is clearly Fiedler's end in view, and it seems to me to represent the chief danger of his position as a whole. Coming to us in the disguise of the disinterested analytical critic, the protector of serious literary values, he is yet an underground campaigner for the new intellectual orthodoxy, for a literature of such sobriety and maturity that to compose it no writer will ever have to leave the warm protection of the bourgeois womb. Near the end of his book he observes with a nearly audible sigh of middle-class contentment that "our writers no longer go to Africa or the left bank to escape from the dullness of America to a world of pure Experience; they are tourists or art historians or government officials or holders of grants and fellowships, but they are not Exiles." It seems to me obvious that the dullness of America is as much if not more of a reality today than it was thirty years ago when the famous exile movement took place, and that if the present generation of American writers are refusing to escape from that dullness, it may be because they have themselves succumbed to it. Certainly one may wonder whether much of the pretentious mediocrity of recent American writing may not be attributed to the fact that it was produced by tourists, art historians, government officials, and fellowship holders rather than by men of genuine talent pursuing "pure Experience" in the immaturity of exile.

But Fiedler's passionate compact with orthodoxy has all the earmarks of a metaphysical *mariage de convenance;* his heart clearly remains with the values he scorns, and his scorn is clearly a defense raised by his pride against the fact of his failure to make those values his own. This is one of the tragedies of the literary generation to which Fiedler belongs: they all in a sense suffer from the trauma inflicted upon them by the decline of Bohemia, the disappearance in their time of the possibility of the free creative life. Their orthodoxy, like that of their political contemporaries, is the other side of their thwarted urge toward heresy, the surrogate form of their disillusioned romanticism, their way of liking what they can get after failing to get what they would have liked. I am thinking of the writers who grew up too late to have an active part in the literary movement of the twenties and thirties but who nevertheless partook of its atmosphere and formed their first attitudes on the views of art and the artist that were fashionable at the time. As a second and entirely spectatorial generation, they were deeply affected by the ideas of exile, iconoclasm, and creative independence on which the movement had been based, and they naturally took as their idols the men who seemed to exemplify these ideas in their purest form, men like Joyce, Lawrence, Pound, Eliot, and Hemingway, who together comprised a sort of cultural-heroic abstraction of the socially alienated but artistically dedicated writer. It was largely on the basis of this abstraction that the younger group formed their view of the writer and the literary life, and it was inevitable that they should sooner or later begin to form a view of their own future purposes as writers on the ideal which it held out. But the world they came into after 1945 was not one in which this ideal any longer had a place or function as a working creative premise. The small coteries with their independent "little" reviews and special audiences, which had encouraged and sustained the older writers in their attitudes of alienation, had by then died out or been corrupted into self-parody; the centers of literary power and prestige had shifted both from the coterie and from the former open market of genteel publishing to the universities, their journals and audiences; and the aging masters of the exile movement had themselves become institutionalized, their private lives turned into topics for research, their best works into standard sophomore texts. The deification of the movement furthermore had led everywhere to a deification of the act of writing, and in the process it had become an act divorced from all impulse, a thing which everybody, regardless of talent or need, had to learn to perform. Writers who had been good writers flocked to the universities to teach writing to students who were taking degrees in the art of being writers—the whole mechanism working at an increasing remove from that primary commitment to experience which first teaches the writer. The few writers, on the other hand, who remained free of the universities and who ought to have served as examples of the efficacy of the literary life, were paradoxically scorned when they were not simply ignored by those who taught, for in spite of all the apparent creative activity, it was generally thought doubtful that anything more of value remained to be done in literature. Besides, the independent writer in a very real sense constituted a threat to the security of the others. He persisted in doing what they lacked the courage and incentive to do; he was a living reminder of the fact that they had once wanted and had perhaps been able to do it. But above all he represented the last obstacle in the path to the final fulfillment of the institutionalizing process, which was the concentration of all literary power within the universities and the creation of a class of men as its legislators who had never written, had never intended to write, but who had been taught by writers exclusively to teach others to write. These men would devote their time to using and dispensing power and to exploiting the advantages accruing to them by virtue of the fact that they were ostensibly literary men, while at the same time they would not be required to take the risks they would have to take if they were really literary men. Against the possibility of such a manufacture, the independent writer stood as a recalcitrant symbol of genuine literary values and of the real world of letters where reputations were made on the basis of risks taken and work accomplished. In the universities, therefore, he was dismissed as a crank and a maverick.

Coming into such a situation the younger intellectuals of Leslie Fiedler's generation who had at one time entertained hopes of following the course of the masters had very little choice but to conform. For the most part, they too lacked the courage and incentive to become independent, but they had had, in any case, such limited experience of life outside the universities and been so steeped in the history of the movement's decline rather than in the metaphysics of its revival that they were not disposed to develop in a creative way. Besides, as their learning increased, the traditional forms and poses of creative action began to seem to them quaint and outmoded: exile was now clearly a dead end; starvation for one's art was no longer in order; rebellion seemed childish and unnecessary; there was no sense in the age of the opening of new literary frontiers; and the social and economic situation was such that everyone wanted marriage, a family, and the amenities, along with the money and security to maintain them. The result was, therefore, that the majority of the group succumbed to the closest existing version of the way of life which they had originally aspired to, and that was the manufactured literary life of the universities. They became teachers of writing and modern literature, and as time went on and their talents atrophied, they too came to hate the independent writer, and finally the whole independent creative tradition which they had formerly worshiped, for they were secretly ashamed of the romantic adolescents they had once been, and even more ashamed of the way they had sold out their adolescent hopes. Their only salvation lay now in protecting the institution, in assenting to the hypocrisies of value with which they had allowed the institution to replace those hopes, and so they began to occupy themselves with problems of academic status, advancement, and tenure; they became critics and scholars, models of Fiedler's orthodox man of maturity.

The careful self-protectiveness behind this pious assent to orthodoxy is nowhere more starkly revealed than in the several articles which have lately appeared on the subject of the movement of the writer to the universities. With the single exception, I believe, of Mr. V. S. Pritchett's short essay not long ago in *The New York Times Book Review*—an essay which, incidentally, was largely critical of the movement—these commentaries have all been written by writers who have themselves gone to the universities, and so one may suspect them of bias. But what is remarkable about them is how baldly, with what a cynical attentiveness to the front row of the baccalaureate gallery, they reveal their bias. They do not argue merely that the university is a good place for the writer to be. They take it for granted that the *only* really important writers are those in the university teaching writing. Over and over again, for example, one sees them elevating Wallace Stegner, Theodore Morrison, Allan Seager, and Mark Schorer—some of whom, to be sure, are competent enough writers—above such men as William Styron, Norman Mailer, Truman Capote, and conceivably even Hemingway and Faulkner, not on the basis of any honest comparison of their respective merits, but simply because the latter happen not to hold memberships in the teaching fraternity. It is of course not hard to understand how this ranking system grew up nor how the general reading public might be led to accept it as the official guide to the assessment of reputations. Until around ten years ago the universities and the academic journals were given over almost entirely to scholars and scholarship, while criticism was in the hands of independent men of letters—men like Edmund Wilson, Van Wyck Brooks, Malcolm Cowley, and the younger Allen Tate and R. P. Blackmur—who were interested mainly in the independent writer. But since that time the most influential centers of critical opinion have been located in the universities and the journals where critics tend to know and to breed only their own kind, and where what little creative work is published is likely to be almost exclusively that of university writers, who, as a rule, lack means of publication elsewhere. The critics and writers who are dependent upon the journals for publication and knowledge of literary affairs are therefore bound to assume that the best writers are those whose interests are most like their own and whose work appears regularly in the journals. Then, by somewhat the same process that has promoted Faulkner and T. S. Eliot to the front covers of *Time,* a kind of low-brow flirtation with the high-brow institutional, it has become the university writers who write the literary surveys and analyses-of-the-year which appear in the popular review media—*The Saturday Review, The New York Times,* and the *New York Herald Tribune*—and which naturally have to do with other university writers, so that the public comes to believe that the universities alone are subsidizing American literature.

Mr. Charles Fenton, a Yale instructor and Hemingway scholar, is one of the newest propagandists for this view. In an article appearing in *New World Writing No. 7* he notes triumphantly that

> . . . this phenomenon of the writer as professor is now a fixed and recurrent one. It is, indeed, no longer a phenomenon; it is fact. A first generation of writer-teachers, men like Theodore Morrison, Wallace Stegner, Robert Penn Warren, Horace Gregory, and Allan Seager, have now attained academic stability. . . . A second generation, far more numerous and, on the whole, less widely known as writers, though no less distinguished, has solidified and extended the invasion. Paul Engle, John Ciardi, Mark Schorer, Richard Wilbur, Peter Viereck, Randall Jarrell, Saul Bellow—all these and many more have consolidated the writers' beachhead in the universities. Now a third generation of young men who want to write are preparing themselves in the graduate schools for the academic assault. . . . Today there is scarcely an English Department in the United States which does not contain a practicing poet or novelist—or short story writer or playwright—who teaches a seminar or two in creative writing, perhaps a course in contemporary American literature, and, maybe, if his position is insecure and his chairman unfriendly, a section of Freshman English.

Fenton's charging military metaphors eloquently proclaim the message which his observations by themselves cannot confirm: that the salvation of American letters by the universities has now been accomplished. The best and most distinguished, albeit "less widely known" writers in the country have come down with a fine, healthy case of pernicious academia. *Requiescat in pace,* all you worriers and dissenters. The situation is well in hand.

Without at all intending to cast doubt upon the truth of the phenomenon Fenton describes or to disparage the talents of the writers he cites as examples of it—although a good case for disparagement might in certain instances be made—I should like to set more definite limits to his argument. Let us consider the university affiliations of some of the writers who automatically come to mind whenever one thinks seriously of contemporary literature. Among the poets who have been more or less regular teachers there are John Ciardi, Paul Engle, Richard Wilbur, Peter Viereck, Randall Jarrell, Karl Shapiro, Robert Lowell, Howard Nemerov, Horace Gregory, John Crowe Ransom, Allen Tate, John Berryman, W. H. Auden, Stephen Spender, and Archibald MacLeish, but of these Tate, Auden, Spender, and MacLeish did not settle permanently upon teaching until fairly late in their careers. Among the poets who are not teachers there are T. S. Eliot, the late Wallace Stevens, William Carlos Williams, Conrad Aiken, E. E. Cummings, and Robinson Jeffers, of whom the most distinguished are in markedly nonacademic professions: Eliot in publishing, Stevens in insurance, and Williams in medicine. The situation of the novelists is strikingly different. Saul Bellow, Robert Penn Warren, Mark Schorer, Wallace Stegner, Theodore Morrison, Randall Jarrell, and Robie Macauley may all be considered university novelists; but the ratio of partial or intermittent employment is somewhat higher among them than it is among the poets. Of the novelists who have never been teachers there are—to mention only the best-known names in a nearly infinite list—Hemingway, Faulkner, Dos Passos, Steinbeck, James Gould Cozzens, James T. Farrell, Carson McCullers, Paul Bowles, William Styron, Truman

Capote, Wright Morris, Gore Vidal, Norman Mailer, Calder Willingham, Irwin Shaw, and James Jones.

These statistics perhaps prove only what one might have suspected: that the majority of the most important older poets and novelists have been able to live without teaching, and when they have needed to work, the older poets at least have chosen other fields; that the more commercially successful of our younger novelists have done likewise; and that it has been mainly the younger group of poets who have had to teach. But certainly this gives us a far different view of the matter from the one circulated by Fenton, and it serves to disprove the primary implication of his remarks that the best of our writers are teachers. It also disproves the argument with which he attempts to make that contention inarguable: that the economic situation of the serious writer is such that he has no choice but to teach. It is of course true that since the decline of patronage there have been almost no poets who have been able to support themselves by their work. Very few of them in our day have been as fortunate even as the distinguished poet whom R. P. Blackmur describes as having devoted his entire time to writing and still never having made more than three thousand in a year, with an average over thirty years of five hundred. But it is evidently still possible, in spite of the shrinkage in advances and reprint sales, for the average good novelist to remain self-supporting. If many novelists are choosing not to do so and are preferring to teach instead, I suspect the reason is not economics but a failure of nerve coupled with a disaffection with the ideal of the independent literary life.

I do not wish, however, to seem unaware of the several distinctions which can and should be made in any sensible ap proach to this problem. One ought to take into account, for example, the difference between the situation of the novelist who published a first book, say, in 1947 and that of one who did not appear with a first book until 1952. The novel of 1947 would undoubtedly have received its due share of critical notice; it most certainly had a chance of at least being read, and the writer of making at least a start on a following and a bank account. At that time everyone was interested in the direction the new postwar literature would take; publishers were touting new novelists; and reviewers were attentive to their work. But the novel published in 1952 came into an atmosphere of saturation and relative indifference; publishers were reducing their promotional outlays for first work; and reviewers had grown perfunctory in their treatment of fiction generally. The novelist, consequently, was likely to find himself published and quickly dropped, without having come within hailing distance of either following or fortune, and with no recourse other than teaching. When I speak here and elsewhere of the younger group of independent novelists, I refer to those who appeared right after the war in the advantageous time and who were fortunate enough to begin their careers in the flush of some financial success which enabled them to become at least temporarily independent of the necessity to take other work or to teach. But an interesting fact about the younger university writers which Mr. Fenton himself acknowledges is that, for the most part, they are not writers who have tried and failed to become independent and have then gone into teaching as a compromise. Rather, they are writers who have gone into teaching directly from college and who have never experienced the struggles of the marketplace.

Mr. Fenton observes that it is this tendency which sets the younger university writers apart from the older. The latter nearly all came to the university after an early career of independent writing and took to teaching as a means of making a living while still retaining the orientation of literary men. The former have had a university orientation from the beginning and tend to look upon writing as the pedants of the old school looked upon formal scholarship, as primarily a means to academic status, fame, and power. Mr. Fenton assumes, nevertheless, that the threat of poverty is the main reason for the movement to teaching, and near the end of his essay he sets out to prove that the necessity for the writer to live by his work imposes a burden upon him which is ultimately smothering to his faculties and which a teaching job would remove. The example he uses is Dylan Thomas, who was badgered to the end of his life by debts and the distractions of petty jobs and who shortly before his death was reduced to begging for a loan of one hundred pounds from a wealthy former patroness. The spectacle is of course pitiable; it is a depressing coda to what we already know to be the tragic story of Dylan Thomas. But what Mr. Fenton seems to forget is that it was undoubtedly the threat of poverty which kept Thomas writing—just as it was the lust for wealth and position that kept Balzac writing—even though from time to time he may have had to set aside his serious work and turn temporary hack. The writer, on the other hand, who goes into teaching is likely to decline in productiveness as the economic pressure upon him is removed; and as he begins to enjoy the status advantages of his position, he is almost certain in the end to lose the need to prove himself as a writer. He now *is* a writer; that is how he came by his teaching job; and he will remain a writer in his own eyes and those of his society without any further writing effort on his part as long as the job lasts. This undoubtedly accounts for the low productivity of the university novelists whom Mr. Fenton mentions. It is one of their distinguishing features as a group that they are nearly all one-book men or men whose books are scattered sparsely over long stretches of time. Since they already inhabit what at least looks like a literary situation, they are relieved of the obligation to create a real one out of their own work. Under the patronage of the university they do not have to count on their writing to do everything for them. Their independent contemporaries, on the other hand, are forced to be fairly regular producers; they have no choice but to pay their tithe to posterity in work accomplished.

That Mr. Fenton's own academic commitments prevent him from recognizing this is made clear in his remarks on the type of writers to whom university life is *not* recommended. These, he says, are

> . . . the writers for whom the academic world would be a catastrophe for reasons of temperament and attitude. The rich, angry vigor of Arthur Miller would be, well, unnecessarily overstimulated by departmental meetings and hierarchical jockeying. There are a few institutions which welcome the professional bohemian, but even the very loose academic structure of Bread Loaf was devastated by Truman Capote; the effect of a fully flowered exotic on an English Department—and it upon him—would be monumental. Nor would a university career seem appropriate for a productive, richly fertile and imaginative popular writer. Stephen Vincent Benét endured

the Yale Graduate School for six months and then fled to Paris. Later he disciplined himself to attend symposiums and give lectures, but he never became thoroughly at ease with the academic requirements. "God did not make me to be an influence," he wrote his wife once from a two-week period of residence in a university writing program. "He meant me to sit on my rear and write."

Mr. Fenton is obviously trying to create the impression here that it is only the freakish and emotionally unstable writer who would not be acceptable in teaching, or, for that matter, anywhere else in polite, respectable society. He makes use of loaded terms like "temperament and attitude," "exotic," and "popular" to fend off the real matter at hand, which is that the writers he mentions would not and could not teach because they are *real* writers. The crucial point is not "temperament and attitude," for there are many other writers without marked idiosyncrasies to whom teaching would be equally disastrous, and for the same reason. Arthur Miller and Truman Capote are, after all, serious, productive writers; Stephen Vincent Benét was a serious, productive, albeit popular writer. As such, their primary concern has been the perfection of their talents and the discovery of the kind of experience, however exotic, which will best provide them with material. They have all been dedicated to sitting on their rears and writing, a feat of spiritual athletics from which most of the university writers have been in frantic flight.

Mr. Donald Hall, in an essay appearing in the same issue of *New World Writing*, speaks of the university writer in a tone of complacent self-protectiveness that is very similar to Mr. Fenton's. After surveying the situation of the younger generation of American poets, nearly all of whom are teachers, Mr. Hall observes that

> . . . poets are ridiculed as teachers: the patronage system established by the universities supports many of the poets I have mentioned. Is there any reason why an opium den is intrinsically more poetic than a Senior Common Room? In this attack is only the romantic cliché of the poet as starving revolutionary—a cliché contradicted by the contemporary poet who lives in a suburb and lectures to undergraduates.

Once again one notices the strenuous effort to fend off the real matter at hand; the use of emotive words and extreme alternatives—"opium den" is opposed to "Senior Common Room" in an unreal, purposely weighted juxtaposition of values; "starving revolutionary" is made the arbitrary synonym for the serious writer; romantic clichés are used to contradict a romantic cliché attack. The real question which Mr. Hall strategically renders rhetorical and senseless is not whether "an opium den is intrinsically more poetic than a Senior Common Room," for the opium den is not, and to my knowledge has never been an alternative to the Senior Common Room. What poet since De Quincey has lived in an opium den? The alternative is the independent creative life, and that is always more poetic than any Common Room. It is so because it is a life dedicated wholly to the values of creative production, not to the manufactured and institutionalized equivalents of those values. One would suppose, furthermore, that there might still be some doubt as to just how thoroughly the lecturing, suburbanite poet of today contradicts the older romantic cliché. The new poet may have all the competence which Mr. Hall attributes to him (at least he ought to have, for he is, above all, a scholar of poetry), but the poets he admires, imitates, and lectures to undergraduates about are still those who, like Yeats, Eliot, Pound, Williams, Auden, and Stevens, lived the free creative life and who, in eschewing the suburbs and the lecture platforms, attained to a poetic vision of the age which he and his contemporaries have not yet been able to equal.

But Hall, Fenton, and Fiedler are all apologists for the new intellectual orthodoxy; they have to be because they are themselves fully committed to it. Mr. Hall's opium den would not be available to him even if he wanted to move in, and of course he does not want to. It is of much greater use to him vacant, for then he can say that nobody wants to rent it; everybody prefers the Senior Common Room. Everybody is right, of course. In the Common Room they risk having none of those clammily distasteful encounters with experience to which they would be subject in the opium den; they enjoy there all the benefits of creative calomel without any of the dangers; and as long as they remain there, they can take advantage of the various emoluments which the Common Room makes available to them in partial recompense, one supposes, for the damage it has done to their chances with posterity. There are, for example, in addition to the normal prizes of status, salary, and tenure, such extra inducements for the university writer as the literary fellowships sponsored by the *Kenyon* and *Sewanee Reviews,* which are both journals edited or controlled by other university writers. These fellowships were made possible through a grant of funds a few years ago from The Rockefeller Foundation and have since been awarded on a yearly basis at the rate of three at a time, one in poetry, one in fiction, and one in criticism. According to the published circulars, the fellowships are intended to stimulate fresh activity in these fields by providing a year's subsidy for young writers of exceptional promise and presumably of some real need. But what the circulars do not state are the qualifications beyond youth, talent, and need which the candidate is expected to possess. After reviewing the lists of successful candidates, however, one can easily deduce them. To receive a fellowship a writer must be either a university teacher of some experience or a fairly regular contributor to the *Kenyon* and *Sewanee Reviews,* preferably both. He must, in other words, be a member of the fraternity. Of the ten *Kenyon* fellows created since the inception of the program in 1953, six were university teachers, one was a recent graduate of Kenyon College, one was Director of Publicity at Kenyon College(!), one was a Junior Fellow at Harvard, one was an independent novelist, and all were contributors to the magazine. This kind of selection was made in spite of the fact that the *Kenyon* editors, in stating their own qualifications for selecting fellows, alluded pridefully to their "professionally wide acquaintance among American writers." It would appear either that they were mistaken or that they sincerely believe—as one suspects they do—that the really important American writers are in the colleges, graduate schools, and campus publicity offices. At any rate, among the nine *Sewanee* fellows created since 1953, the record was perfect: all were academics, and all were contributors. As to the quality of the fellows themselves one can only express an opinion. All we officially know about them is that they are supposed to be "distinguished younger writers." They include Flannery O'Connor, George Lanning, Howard Nemerov, Edwin Watkins, Irving Howe, William S. Merwin, R. W. B. Lewis, Richard Ellman, Edgar Bogardus, Douglas Nichols, Louis D. Rubin, Jr., Danforth Ross, Edgar Bowers, James L. Dickey, Madison Jones, John Hardy, Mac Hammond, Louis Coxe, and Walter Sullivan. Of these Flannery O'Connor and Howard Nemerov in fiction, Irving Howe, R. W. B. Lewis, and Richard Ellman in criticism, and Louis Coxe and William S. Merwin in poetry have produced work ranging in quality from competence to excellence. A little of it, but only a very little, might be called distinguished. Miss O'Connor and Mr. Nemerov are decidedly minor younger novelists, even among younger novelists; Messrs. Howe, Lewis, and Ellman, on the other hand, are as promising as any critics of the generation now about forty; Mr. Merwin, to my mind, is for his age a poet of real stature. But nearly all of the others are virtually unknown outside the quarterlies; some of them are barely known even within them; and all are represented by only a few poems and scattered short stories. It might be said, in short, that while they are probably on the average all good enough people, they scarcely constitute a fair sampling of the best younger talent in the country, the kind of fair sampling which the quarterlies in their present positions of power and influence ought to be able to make and ought to take pains to make, particularly when they are spending the funds of a national foundation.

But quality is obviously not a major factor in the selection of fellows. What is far more crucial is the extent to which the candidates, having met the official requirements, are able to meet the various others imposed by the political interests of the quarterlies themselves. These are all extremely complex and hard to define, but it is possible at least to observe them in action and to point to their influence in specific cases. Miss Flannery O'Connor, for example, is, as I have said, a distinctly minor novelist; yet she alone of all the fellows has enjoyed the honor of receiving two *Kenyon* awards in fiction. The reason presumably is that Miss O'Connor has lately become the official "younger Southern novelist" of the quarterlies. Her fiction has to do, in the main, with simple Southern peasant folk set against rustic Southern backgrounds, and for the academic Northern intellectual what is Southern and rustic is synonymous with all that is original, serious, and true in American letters. In a sense, Miss O'Connor does for the academic intellectuals what Truman Capote does for the pseudo intellectuals of the flossy New York fashion-magazine world—she provides them with tone or chic, a little sprinkling of fake old magnolia blossoms; she is the literary equivalent of the Grand Rapids–Modern spider furniture which they display in their living rooms along with the work of the most recently modish, obscure nineteenth-century Provençal painter. Miss O'Connor has therefore won a high place in the hall of quarterly fame. Another Southern novelist, equally young and infinitely more talented, Mr. William Styron, would not, on the other hand, fare so well; in fact, it is doubtful if he would fare at all, although it is not a matter of public record whether he has ever been invited to apply for a quarterly fellowship. Mr. Styron's *Lie Down in Darkness* is easily the most distinguished Southern novel of the present decade, his *The Long March* one of the two or three distinguished novelettes of the last thirty years. Yet Mr. Styron would be disqualified for membership in the *Kenyon-Sewanee* hierarchy of "distinguished younger writers" on two serious counts: he has never published a word in either magazine, and he is crass enough to have enjoyed a certain small commercial success through his writings. By the same token, Mr. Saul Bellow, another outstanding younger novelist, would be excluded, for although he had at one time a very high standing in the quarterlies, both as a frequent contributor and as a subject of commentary, he has lately lost caste because of the popular success of *The Adventures of Augie March* and because he is suspected of devoting himself a bit too exclusively to "creative" work, a practice looked upon as somewhat beneath the serious intellectual mind. With the appearance of his fairly widely read novel *Pictures from an Institution* and his critical book *Poetry and the Age* Mr. Randall Jarrell, also a long-time quarterly favorite, appears to be about to suffer the same fate; one sees his articles now in *Mademoiselle* and *The New York Times Book Review*, and it is almost as if one had encountered him down and out on Skid Row.

In the areas of criticism and poetry the qualifications of institutional affiliation required of the fellowship candidate are even more rigid. The young critic ought, first of all, to be a scholar, preferably with a doctor's degree, and he ought, secondly, to be working within the new critical tradition, the tradition from which *The Sewanee Review*, somewhat late in its history, and *The Kenyon Review* from its beginnings received their guiding impetus. The present editors of both reviews—Allen Tate, Francis Fergusson, John Crowe Ransom, and Cleanth Brooks—all grew up in this tradition and won their early reputations by championing its cause in the face of the genteel romantic criticism of their day. But these men do not require of their younger contemporaries a similar rebelliousness; in fact, they do their best to discourage it. The present-day versions of themselves would be writing for present-day versions of the old *Kenyon* and *Sewanee Reviews*—if such existed—and these would, by definition, be severely critical of the present *Kenyon* and *Sewanee Reviews*. The new young Allen Tate, therefore, would hardly be awarded a fellowship. But luckily for them, the young candidates in criticism have shown no inclination to rebel. They have confined themselves to good, sound, scholarly works of research and exegesis, for they have known that only by conforming could they hope to move up through the successive stages of the critical life cycle into which the sanction of their elders could be expected to launch them—the cycle beginning with a *Kenyon* or *Sewanee* fellowship, running through a Christian Gauss lectureship at Princeton, a teaching appointment at one of the better Eastern universities, a place on the staff of the Indiana School of Letters, and ending in final triumph with an advisory editorship on the *Kenyon* or *Sewanee Review*. The candidates in poetry also anticipate a cyclical development, although it is better for them if they have completed as much of their cycle as possible before coming up for an award. Their cycle begins, as a rule, with graduation from one of the better Eastern universities and runs through a Rhodes scholarship or comparable work at Oxford, graduate study, a junior fellowship at Harvard, a *Kenyon* or *Sewanee* fellowship, a teaching appointment at one of the better Eastern universities, a Guggenheim fellowship, a Consultantship in Poetry at the Library of Congress, a place on the staff of the Indiana School of Letters, to an advisory editorship on the *Kenyon* or *Sewanee Review*. The only awards the skillful fellowship holder does not sooner or later find himself automatically in line for are the Pulitzer and the Nobel prizes, the one because it is given in part for popularity, the other because it is given almost wholly for achievement.

The Guggenheim fellowship program has traditionally been the sole source of patronage available to the independent younger writer. Yet contrary to the prevailing belief both in the public at large and among writers themselves, the Guggenheim Foundation has never done very much for the independent writer, young or old. From the time of its creation in 1925, its fellowship program has been principally devoted to the support of scholarly research projects in the sciences and humanities, although in a statement issued that year Simon Guggenheim said that the program was intended "to improve the quality of education *and* the practice of the arts and professions in the United States," and there has regularly been a clause in the official prospectus to the effect that the aim has been "to further the development of scholars *and artists* by assisting them to engage in research in any field of knowledge and artistic creation in any of the fine arts including music, under the freest possible conditions." It was apparently very much on Mr. Guggenheim's mind in the beginning that talented young men and women right out of college were being forced into teaching without first having the opportunity to engage, as he put it, in "creative work in their subjects," and it was his intention that the fellowships would be used primarily to provide them with such an opportunity. He also clearly intended the program to perform a similar service for younger creative artists, although the emphasis was initially placed on scholarship, and this emphasis has determined policy ever since. There is much evidence to indicate, however, that as the years have passed the program has gradually been transformed into something far different from what Mr. Guggenheim envisioned, and that it has all but abdicated its stated obligations to younger scholars and artists. Before the twenties had ended, the age limits of twenty-five to thirty-five originally set for candidates had been revised upwards to forty, and since then the revision has continued, until now the upper limit, while still officially only forty, is in practice apparently located somewhere in the hinterlands of senility. More and more scholars of all the mature ages have received fellowships with less and less regard for whether their projects have been creative, and the proportion of awards made to artists of whatever age has sharply declined. In 1932, 11 per cent of the total fellowships awarded went to creative writers alone; in 1933 writers made up 24 per cent of the total; in 1937, 11 per cent; in 1949, 6 per cent; in 1952, 5 per cent; in 1954, 3 per cent; and in 1955, 3 per cent. This decline has occurred in spite of the fact that the number of fellowships awarded has risen from forty or fifty in 1925 to 234 in 1955. Since the end of World War II, moreover, the Ford Foundation and the Fulbright program have opened vast new sources of subsidy for scholars, so that their need for Guggenheim support has been greatly diminished, while scholars in the scientific fields now have ready access to research funds provided by private industry and the Federal government. Once again, it is the independent writer, living from book to book without even the minimal security of an academic salary, who is forced to suffer.

One is tempted to conclude that the reason for this is that the members of the Guggenheim Selection Committee have succumbed to the prevailing belief that a writer is no good unless he is a professor, hence within the category of automatic subsidy. But it is much more likely that, since all the committee members are themselves professors, they just naturally prefer other professors, particularly older ones like themselves. When confronted with writers they obviously feel uneasy and rather out of depth. While fellowship winners in the other arts are chosen by a special advisory committee made up of professional workers in those arts, the writers are chosen by the regular committee, with the result that the selections tend as a rule to be somewhat ambiguous and erratic, ranging from one or two people of indisputable talent to several people of little or none. This is especially lamentable when dozens, perhaps hundreds, of good writers apply and are turned down annually. I know of one young writer, author of five serious novels and a distinguished play, who has applied and been turned down four times running. Another applied with the highest recommendations from some of the most respected men in his field and still was refused. What the Guggenheim Foundation desperately needs of course is an advisory committee composed of serious young writers, but to bring that about one would first have to scotch the cherished academic myth that a professor may be totally ignorant of the other arts but is always competent to judge the art of writing.

As for the scholarly projects which the Selection Committee deem worthy of subsidy in such numbers, it is difficult to speak of some of them without collapsing into burlesque. One cannot help wondering if such matters as "Trade in the ancient

Mediterranean as documented by stamped wine jars," "The legal rights of employees within Swedish labor unions," "The fungi of the Society Islands," "Studies in the history of the theory of the rainbow," "The auxiliaries of the Roman imperial army," "Studies of the anatomy of the Old World species of onions," and "French émigrés to Schleswig-Holstein" could really have been considered by the Committee to be creative enough and important enough to merit the awards which were made for them in 1954 and 1955. But T. S. Eliot perhaps gave the answer when he said:

> We assume . . . that we are masters and not servants of facts, and that we know that the discovery of Shakespeare's laundry bills would not be of much use to us; but we must always reserve final judgment as to the futility of the research which has discovered them, in the possibility that some genius will appear who will know of a use to which to put them.

It would seem that at least some of the Guggenheim scholars are engaged in the accumulation of laundry bills, and until the genius appears who will vindicate them in the enterprise, I see no reason for supposing it of greater intrinsic value to the world than the creative survival of a single gifted young writer.

In view of all this, it would appear that the American university today holds out to the writer an abundance of advantages, by which it would be less than human of him not to be strongly tempted. In addition to the opportunity for fellowship support and the normal academic rewards of security and status, it offers him membership in a closely knit, highly selective intellectual class, in which, if he obeys the rules, he will be able to spend the rest of his life in the company of friends and peers. This is not so simple as it sounds, for it does not mean merely that the writer in the university enjoys the close fraternity of a professional group with interests congenial to his own. It means that in the university he becomes part of a vast and complex social organism which very largely *is* the literary-intellectual life of America today. The academic world and the literary world are, for all practical purposes, synonymous in this country at the present time. The universities control literature, its agencies, and its functions in a manner and to a degree that have been unparalleled in Western culture since at least the eighteenth century. Not even the immensely powerful group movements of the more recent past—those at Bloomsbury, Oxford, Paris, Chicago, and New York—have been remotely as influential, for the power of the universities today is not a localized power; there is no activity however faintly literary that is not touched by it. The cultural life of New York, in both its central and its marginal activities relating to literature, is dominated by university professors: they edit and comprise the bulk of the contributors to the leading intellectual magazines; they make up the boards of directors of the philanthropic foundations; they serve as advisers to publishers, edit, and write introductions for books; they act as technical consultants and cultural performers in radio and television. The poems, stories, and novels that are most discussed are nearly always those which have first received endorsement in academic circles and which very often have been written by professors. Where at one time it was the independent writer, a Dreiser, an Anderson, a Thomas Wolfe, who occupied the seat of honor at intellectual gatherings, whose opinions carried the most weight with publishers and editors, it is now the man from Harvard or Columbia, the critic with the lead essay in the current *Partisan* or the lead poem. If literary reputations are made anywhere today, they are made among professors, and they are kept alive or allowed to perish by professors. It is probably no exaggeration to say that the best and most serious elements of the modern cultural movement, including all aspects of experiment and technical innovation as well as the properties of taste required to evaluate them, are now and have been for years under the sole custodianship of professors. There is simply nowhere else for them to be. The professor is the new cultural force, the leader, and god of the new aristocracy of the intellect.

Therein lies, it seems to me, the principal danger for the writer as professor. He inhabits a professional world crowded with daily reminders of his remarkable preeminence. His contacts with his students afford him a constantly renewing sense of creative fulfillment; his station in his class places at his disposal quantities of influence; his regular preoccupation is with literary values and judgments. In time he is likely to lose sight of the fact that the university is at best only a manufacture of a literary situation, an institutional construct raised over the dead forms of creative impulses, and to begin confusing the quasi satisfactions which he gets from the university with the real satisfactions which he can get only from rigorous application to his own work. But everything in his life operates to foment that confusion, for so long as teaching makes him feel that he is a writer and engaging in literary problems, so long as he enjoys as a teacher the authority and influence that would come to him as a writer, he will not be impelled to function as a writer. Besides, perhaps without being aware of it, he daily suffers a breakdown in the integrity of his writing consciousness. He makes use in the classroom of insights and emotions which he ought to be using in his writing, so that if and when he comes back to writing he tends to experience a crippling sense of having said it all before, of being about to commit self-plagiarism. He is also likely to find that only in a nominal way does he inhabit a literary community, that most of his colleagues are indifferent if not downright hostile to literary values, and that, as far as his physical environment is concerned, it seems to have no connection with him whatever. If he teaches at one of the larger Middle Western universities, he will probably come to feel that he is inhabiting a cultural outpost, a veritable arsenal of learning, in the middle of a wasteland hundreds of miles from the centers of art and literature, and that in spite of his professional prestige, as an ordinary man he is living among barbarians and peasants. He thus begins to suffer a second derangement, this time a derangement of his sense of the external world. He can neither accept that world nor wholly reject it; its values are not his, yet they are all he has coming in; so he anesthetizes himself against it as best he can, and cuts himself off from the emotional nourishment which he needs for himself and his writing. If, on the other hand, he assents to his predicament, denies that it is a predicament, and settles down to convince himself of its virtue, he risks moral suicide, for the lies told for the sake of expediency become, for the writer, the cancers of conscience. If he persists in holding out against it, he risks going sterile and losing the thing which gave him his reason for persisting. If he escapes it altogether, he may yet be saved, but he opens himself to the gravest risk of all, the risk of coming to grips with his talent under the cold, pitiless gaze of posterity.*

* Since I am myself a writer who has gone to the university, I want to make my position plain. I have been a university teacher for several years and expect to continue as one. But I do not see that any purpose is served in attempting to make a virtue of the necessity which impelled me to teaching nor in remaining blind to the many dangers inhering in it for the writer. I am specifically concerned in this essay, however, with the tendency now rapidly accelerating in the intellectual world to endow the university with creative powers and advantages which it does not and cannot possess, and I am particularly opposed to the development which has made the university the seat of literary politics and power in our time and which has transformed so many of our younger intellectuals into university apologists and literary politicians.

THREE

The heresy of literary manners *

WHEN WE SPEAK of manners in the novel, I take it we have in mind something more than the merely fashionable and something less than the merely fastidious. All those occasions on which the term has been used with opprobrium or forced into a loaded synonymity with Mme. de Staël's ceremonials at

* To be properly understood, this essay should be viewed in the context of discussion and rather fierce debate which constitutes both its area of reference and the occasion for its polemical tone. The discussion, centering in *Partisan Review* and the articles in recent years of certain of the editors, has had to do with the question of literary values and manners, their meaning and importance in the development, specifically, of American fiction. In its course, certain statements relating to the question made by Mr. Lionel Trilling, myself, and others have been criticized and debated. It has seemed to me that many of these statements have been misinterpreted and, in some cases, grotesquely misapplied by the commentators, and that a further clarifying statement from me has been called for. This essay represents an attempt at both a clarification and an extension of my views, made in the face of arguments relating literary manners to everything from drawing-room etiquette to an undemocratic affirmation of class snobbery. I am hopeful that it will help to indicate the extent to which such arguments have been uninformed.

court, Mrs. Vanderbilt's hypocrisies at tea, or Mr. Eliot's "pleasing archaeological reconstructions," we must now assume to have been improper occasions, the work not of disinterested minds but of those in whom the very suggestion of manners evokes nightmares of class distinction and minority group, pogrom and ghetto, and whose willed misunderstanding of their meaning is politically requisite to a continued rational engagement of contemporary life, the preservation of what we tend to think of as the liberal-egalitarian or "whole" view of reality.

I would suppose that the whole view, which opposes all social and class distinctions, is precisely the one least calculated to yield up a satisfactory view either of reality or manners, simply because in the hands of its recent proponents it has shown itself to be no view at all, but a pathological refusal to make those distinctions which must be made before any view becomes possible. One can in fact say that the whole view is, by its very nature, a symptom of the actual disappearance of distinctions in all areas of our cultural and intellectual life. A recognition of this disappearance as a fact to be lamented is a necessary first step toward an understanding of the meaning of manners in both literature and the social world; but it is a step which the rigidity of his doctrine will not permit the whole-viewer to take. For him, distinctions of whatever kind are real only to the extent that he can come at them traumatically, within the context of the great social revolution which, in the last century, has been working for their overthrow; and it is in the nature of his political commitment that he should suppose not merely that that revolution is still in progress but that it is fast reaching a victorious end in the achievement of a classless and equalitarian America. This kind of America is the chauvinist dream of the intellectual Left, in the service of which—now that it is almost a reality—the Left has already begun to abandon revolution in order to take up a protective and Rightist position over its fruits. What the fruits are to be protected from is quite simply distinctions, distinctions of class, economy, and privilege, all of which have disappeared, or effectively disappeared, as a result of the revolution but which the whole-viewer is continually afraid will be reimposed. Thus manners, which he interprets as the etiquette-distinctions of privilege, seem to him a threat of the very first magnitude. They are seen, in his terms, as inseparable from the idea of class; the idea of class is seen as inseparable from the idea of a suppressed minority; the idea of a suppressed minority is seen as inseparable from the idea of the totalitarian state; and the idea of the totalitarian state is seen as inseparable from the idea of totalitarian atrocity. One consequently finds oneself brought around the traumatic circle of the whole view to the ghetto and pogrom once again and to the *Caine Mutiny* spectacle of somebody's old-world mother being melted down into soap to be used for washing the backs of dictators.

It would seem then that in searching out a sensible approach to the question of manners in the novel one would do better to cultivate the company of those whose maternal forebears suffered merely the boredom of an unredeemed Middle Western gentility or, at worst, some momentary humiliation at the hands of General Sherman's Light Horse. The traumas inflicted by totalitarian atrocity and by General Sherman may not, in the first instance, be very different; but the variance in the degree of their application to politics, and in the forms which in politics they tend to assume, is infinitely wide. The one ends in a politics of craven receptivity to each slightest stirring of the democratic impulse, wherever and under whatever conditions it may be felt. That is the price atrocity always exacts from its victims before it kills them—abject gratitude for the right simply to remain alive up to the secret hour ordained for death. The other—perhaps because it is historically more remote—asserts itself in a stauncher politics, one that can afford to bargain because it knows that some brands of democracy are better than others and that for some it is possible to pay a higher price than life. The one issues from a psychotic necessity always to count our gains because our losses are too grisly to contemplate. The other issues from an equally psychotic necessity always to count our losses because our gains are too grisly to contemplate. The one measures our gains in the degree of our distance from the pogrom and ghetto. The other measures our losses in the degree of our distance from the truly human. The one is a politics of the whole view because it is backed by a knowledge of the atrocity that can be perpetrated in the name of distinctions. The other is a politics of the parochial view because it is backed by a knowledge of what can be lost when distinctions disappear.

Mr. Eliot, Mr. Tate, Mr. Robert Penn Warren, and the other leading proponents of the parochial view all know what we mean by manners because this latter knowledge constitutes the formative fact of their experience and the controlling bias of their intelligence. It does not matter that Mr. Eliot arrived at it by traversing the swamp of pre-Christian ritual and ascending the rock of the English church or that Mr. Tate and Mr. Warren came by it only because they could not get the thundering hoofbeats of Sherman's Light Horse out of their heads. It does not even matter that between the church, Sherman, and the modern world there seems, for the rest of us today, to be no immediate or necessary connection. The single distorted image can sometimes speak to us in the full language of its genre, and we do not need to know the whole of reality (nor can we know it) if we know well the ground we stand on. For Mr. Eliot, Mr. Tate, and Mr. Warren, the church and Sherman are simply aberrations of vision. They are partial, distorted, and blinding; consequently, they make vision possible. They are what happens to vision when it retreats behind something in order to see; it sees less but less more clearly and, because it is protected, it is not obliged to like everything it sees. Mr. Eliot's Anglo-Catholicism and the early Agrarianism of Mr. Tate and Mr. Warren may be considered the ideological abutments behind which their vision has retreated from a reality it has not liked but with which the whole view, as it has gathered force, has sought increasingly to make them content, the reality of a world where the human condition has been abdicated and where the forms of dramatic conduct—what Susanne K. Langer meant, in part, by the term "charged symbols"—have been lost. In one way or another, each of these men has undertaken to say in precisely what this condition and these forms consist and in what circumstances their loss is likely to result. Mr. Eliot throughout his career has spoken frequently of tradition and, in esthetic terms, of structure and convention—"any form or rhythm imposed upon the world of action" that will "arrest, so to speak, the flow of spirit at any particular point before it expands and ends its course in the desert of exact likeness to the reality which is perceived by the most commonplace mind." One has only to substitute "human conduct" for "world of action" to appreciate the ease with which esthetic convention calls to mind its moral and sociological counterpart. Mr. Tate in his essay "What Is a Traditional Society?" has said:

> In ages which suffer the decay of manners, religion, morals, codes, our indestructible vitality demands expression in violence and chaos; . . . men who have lost both the higher myth of religion and the lower myth of historical dramatization have lost the forms of human action . . . they are no longer capable of defining a human objective, of forming a dramatic conception of human nature; they capitulate from their human role to a series of pragmatic conquests which, taken alone, are true only in some other world than that inhabited by men.

And Mr. Warren has suggested that Faulkner's objection to the modern world is that it lacks the ability to set up "codes, concepts of virtue, obligations" by which man can "define himself as human," "realize himself in terms of his whole nature," and "accept the risks of his humanity." Whether one chooses Mr. Eliot's "desert of exact likeness" or Mr. Tate's "other world than that inhabited by men" or Mr. Warren's image of Faulkner's dehumanized world, each represents an assessment of the modern condition opposite to the one provided by the whole view, and each insists on the need for those restraining and defining forms, structures, rituals, patterns, and conventions of conduct which, in the imprisonment of its paranoia, the whole view is committed to denounce as totalitarian heresy.

Even Mr. Lionel Trilling, whose allegiance to the whole view is fortunately qualified by his deeper allegiance to the whole of the Western liberal-humanistic tradition, has recognized the necessity for the existence within a culture of forms and structures such as these and, in so doing, has repeatedly been attacked by those who, having always thought of him as one of themselves, could only conceive of his position as treasonous. In fact, it was Mr. Trilling who first, so far as I know, made explicit the connection between their presence in a culture and the presence in the novel of elements which we customarily take to be the ingredients of dramatic life. Summarizing his sense of these forms and structures in the metaphorical and rather heavily emotive terms "class" and "manners," he has said in his "Art and Fortune" essay:

> In this country the real basis of the novel has never existed—that is, the tension between a middle class and an aristocracy which brings manners into observable relief as the living representation of ideals and the living comment on ideas. . . . If American novels of the past, whatever their merits of intensity and beauty, have given us very few substantial or memorable people, this is because one of the things which makes for substantiality of character in the novel is precisely the notation of manners, that is to say, of class traits modified by personality. . . . American fiction has nothing to show like the huge, swarming, substantial population of the European novel, the substantiality of which is precisely a product of a class existence. In fiction, as perhaps in life, the conscious realization of social class, which is an idea of great power and complexity, easily and quickly produces intention, passion, thought, and what I am calling substantiality. The diminution in the reality of social class . . . seems to have the practical effect of diminishing our ability to see people in their difference and specialness.

Class, as Mr. Trilling conceives it here, is of course only one of the forms which a culture's drives and preoccupations may take, and for a full understanding of the meaning of manners, which he defines in an earlier essay as "a culture's hum and buzz of implication," it is undoubtedly necessary to take into account the more concrete, though less specifically sociological, insights of Mr. Eliot, Mr. Tate, and Mr. Warren. But what is important is that, through the seriousness of their combined approaches, these men have succeeded in elevating the question of manners to a level far above the merely chauvinist vigilantism of the whole view, to a level where it may be recognized for what it really is—an esthetic question of the widest possible pertinence to the dramatics of the novel, both historically and at the present time.

The most recent discussion of manners in the novel—Mr. Delmore Schwartz's in an essay called "The Duchess' Red Shoes" published in *Partisan Review* for January-February, 1953—was vitiated by its willful failure to take account of the question at any recognizable level of seriousness. At least one supposes the failure to have been willful, to have been compelled, this is to say, by Mr. Schwartz's prior commitment to the whole view, which blinded him to all except the most pejorative senses in which the idea of manners may be applied to culture. This, at any rate, is the charitable view of his performance.

But beyond charity there is another reason for granting him the honesty of his impulses. Mr. Schwartz is an editor of *Partisan Review,* a critic of promise, and a poet of some stature. He has a certain reputation in the intellectual world and a certain authority. In the past his opinions have been received by his peers for the most part with that tacit politeness which, if it does not necessarily imply that they have always been respected, at least implies that they have been found to possess the minimum merit requisite to be taken seriously. Since no storm of indignation or rebuttal followed on his discussion of manners, one must assume that in this instance he was again taken seriously, that his observations were generally accepted as fulfilling the requirements of intelligence and good taste laid down for observations of their kind and that, furthermore, they were accorded hospitality by at least the less discriminating of his peers. One may therefore fairly appoint Mr. Schwartz the spokesman for a body of existing, though unarticulated opinion and conceive of his performance as fairly illustrating the level of thought on which ideas of an abstract nature may be acceptably explored among intellectuals today.

The very first sentence of Mr. Schwartz's essay betrays his uneasiness before what he obviously feels to be the personal as well as ideological threat implicit in the subject of manners. "Good manners," he says, "are very pleasant and literary criticism is often very *inn*eresting, to be colloquial. When, however, manners become a major concept in literary criticism, that is something else again: it is an *inn*eruption, to be colloquial again." Taken on the first level, this deliberate descent to bad grammar represents one of the oldest and cheapest tricks known to rhetoric—the attempt to disarm one's opponent by employing low linguistic comedy to disparage the seriousness of his subject or to make it appear pompous. When the subject is manners, which Mr. Schwartz has vested interests in thinking of as "good" manners, it thus becomes a stroke of the sharpest subtlety to open an attack by making burlesque use of bad manners and bad grammar, in quite the same way that small boys express their feelings of inferiority and boredom in polite adult society by covertly sticking out their tongues, wiggling their ears, and making obscene gestures. But the obvious uneasiness one senses in the tone of Mr. Schwartz's remarks forces one to find in them deeper and more serious implications. His bad grammar is not merely a rhetorical trick—for, after all, there is as yet no debate—but a way of further reducing the subject through an appeal to the new intellectual anti-intellectualism, the high-brow equivalent of the fear of ideas and distinctions which, in egghead and middle-brow circles, has taken the form of contrived affability and a tense avoidance of argumentative tension. Ezra Pound exploited this kind of anti-intellectualism to great effect in his correspondence, and for many of the same reasons that Mr. Schwartz exploits it here. Bad grammar for Pound was a subconscious expression of his contempt for his chosen medium and of his desire to place himself on terms of easy fraternity with his friends. Bad grammar for Mr. Schwartz is a somewhat less subconscious expression of *his* contempt for his chosen medium—as Mr. Paul Ramsey specifically charged in his rebuttal letter in *Partisan Review,* May-June, 1953—and of his effort to win over his audience by waving in their faces what Allen Tate, in commenting on Mr. Schwartz's essay, called "the red herring of snobbery." What both Pound and Mr. Schwartz are in effect saying is: "By God, we're all just a bunch of ignorant bums here and, by God, we're proud of it. At least we're *men* and not sissies!" Thus in his first sentence

Mr. Schwartz transforms what might have been a serious discussion of a serious literary issue into a crassly emotive smear involving deeply submerged and highly complicated status drives and taboos—including even the highly suspect masculine taboo against the seemingly effeminate—in his readers as well as in himself.

Mr. Schwartz's subsequent outburst—"Yes, we have no bananas. But all God's chillun got shoes"—is a further development of this approach; and when it is taken in conjunction with the closing paragraph of his reply to Mr. Ramsey, which was published in *Partisan Review* for May-June, 1953, there can no longer be any doubt as to the quality of his thinking or the sincerity of his motives. In this paragraph Mr. Schwartz abandons all pretensions to subtlety and panders to the lowest patriotic and conformist prejudices of his audience.

> My chief reason [he says] for writing as I did was, I think, because I do believe in literature, and in the social ideal proposed by the Constitution, and often violated or unrealized. And also I believe that the future of literature, as of civilization, depends to some important extent upon the realization of that social and human ideal. And finally Mr. Ramsey finds the style of my essay coy, flip, irrelevant, and precious at times. He may be right, but here too *being an American* [the italics are mine] is relevant. Humor is a very important part of American life and often the best way to get other Americans to listen to you, which is the reason I naturally find myself using humor in writing criticism and in responding to critics. Thus, I am merely *fulfilling the obligations of being an American* [the italics are again mine] in trying to be funny, just as, for the same reasons in part, I am trying to be truly an American in owning two used cars, in owning a TV set, in expecting everyone to love me, and in expecting everyone to admire my work and my 1949

Buick. I have also been a loyal Giant fan since 1921. This avowal of fact may explain very little to Mr. Ramsey. It explains a great deal to me and surely it will to other readers.

We may pass over such questions as why Mr. Schwartz feels Americans have to be funny, why he feels he himself has to try so hard to be both funny and American, and why he and so many other liberal intellectuals have felt called upon recently to protest their patriotism in terms which only the American Legion would understand and only Senator McCarthy would fully endorse. We may also pass over, although less easily, the tone of coy self-deprecation and inverted snobbery implicit in his enumeration of his middle-class material assets as well as the interesting fact that he is making a most strenuous appeal to snobbery of one kind in the name of an attack on snobbery of another kind. We may even ignore his final appeal over Mr. Ramsey's head to the red-blooded, baseball-loving Americanism of his readers. But what must bring us up short is his naked admission of a truth which has long been obvious but which has never before been made explicit in his own words: that his fear of the concept of manners, hence his psychological incapacity to deal with it as an esthetic concept, is based on his feeling that it has behind it some odious political doctrine threatening to the Constitution of the United States. Mr. Ramsey's "descending ladder of meanings," down which he has traced the frantic flight of Mr. Schwartz's logic from manners to good manners to snobbery to brutal and insane selfishness, may now be extended beyond brutal and insane selfishness to authoritarianism to totalitarianism to fascism and communism until at last we are brought back again to the suppression of minorities and the pogrom and ghetto—all hallucinated and distorted by the paranoia of the whole view.

By the end of the first section of his essay this compelled and ritualistic association of charged ideas becomes the fixed habit of Mr. Schwartz's discourse, so that all his subsequent observations appear like a series of desperate military maneuvers undertaken in defense of life, liberty, and the pursuit of happiness. This is particularly true of his efforts to preserve the sanctity of the American novel in the face of what he conceives to be aspersions cast by Mr. Trilling. In "Manners, Morals, and the Novel" Mr. Trilling began by defining manners as

> . . . a culture's hum and buzz of implication . . . the whole evanescent context in which its explicit statements are made. It is that part of a culture which is made up of half-uttered or unutterable expressions of value. They are hinted at by small actions, sometimes by the arts of dress or decoration, sometimes by tone, gesture, emphasis, or rhythm, sometimes by the words that are used with a special frequency or a special meaning. They are the things that for good or bad draw the people of a culture together and that separate them from the people of another culture. They make the part of a culture which is not art, or religion, or morals, or politics, and yet it relates to all these highly formulated departments of culture. It is modified by them; it modifies them; it is generated by them; it generates them. In this part of culture assumption rules, which is often so much stronger than reason.
>
> This [says Mr. Schwartz] is Mr. Trilling's broad definition of manners. Throughout his essay, however, he sometimes uses a limited and very different definition of manners, namely, the manners of particular social classes and groups in a given social hierarchy. It is by moving back and forth between his broad (and tentative) definition and his limited (and unexpressed) definition that Mr.

Trilling is able to hold forth *Don Quixote* as a true novel (here the broad definition works) while *The Scarlet Letter* (here it is the limited definition) suffers "from a lack of social texture" and is, like almost all American novels, not concerned with society at all. How can one say, in terms of Mr. Trilling's broad definition, that *The Scarlet Letter, Moby Dick,* and *Huckleberry Finn* lack social texture? The equivalent would be to say that *Walden* is not about society because it deals with a solitary individual. In the same way, again, it is only by using his limited definition and ignoring his broad one that Mr. Trilling can quote and agree with James Fenimore Cooper and Henry James on "the thick social texture of English life and the English novel" in the nineteenth century as opposed to the thinness of American life and the American novel; for in terms of his broad definition there was just as much social texture in America as in England; it was a different social texture as it was a different society and it was not the kind of social texture that James was interested in; but it had just as much of "a culture's hum and buzz of implication," etc., which Mr. Trilling says he means by manners.

Mr. Schwartz's dialectic here is complicated but not impenetrable. His strategy is quite simply to attribute to Mr. Trilling a definition of manners (the limited or "unexpressed" definition) which, in fact, Mr. Trilling never makes, then to show him as shifting confusedly between it and the definition (the broad definition) which he does make, and, finally, to show him as hoist on his own petard by arguing sophistically that this latter definition is invalid because it may be applied to any culture whatever. This is to say that any culture, by reason of the fact that it *is* a culture, will manifest a "hum and buzz of implication," hence, any culture, whether Pueblo Indian or Kwakiutl, has the same supply of manners as any other. The only difference in manners from culture to culture is a difference in kind. Thus, according to Mr. Schwartz, it is impossible to say, as Mr. Trilling does, that, in comparison with nineteenth-century England, nineteenth-century America lacked social texture; it simply had a different social texture, a different kind of manners, but one equally good for the novelist. By means of this process of specious inference, badly disguised as logical demolition, Mr. Schwartz endeavors to direct attention away from Mr. Trilling's real point, which is that there is a valid sense in which it can be argued that there *was* something lacking in the social texture of nineteenth-century America, that in some cultures the "hum and buzz of implication" *is* louder, more irritating, and more various than in others, and that a Kwakiutl culture, by reason of the complexity of its observed manners and the depth of their implication, will always serve the novelist at least potentially better than a Pueblo culture dedicated to the suppression of manners and the cultivation of uniformity.

An acceptance of these propositions makes it possible for one to deal effectively—although, in Mr. Schwartz's terms, heretically—with each of the questions he raises both in the section of his essay just quoted and in the section which follows immediately after it. "How can one say," he asks, "in terms of Mr. Trilling's broad definition, that *The Scarlet Letter, Moby Dick,* and *Huckleberry Finn* lack social texture? The equivalent would be to say that *Walden* is not about society because it deals with a solitary individual." It seems to me that one can say this quite easily. It is because these novels lack social texture, or the society out of which they were written lacked it, that they have to be so strenuously *about* something, that they have to depend for such a large part of their dramatic existence upon the concrete physical event—the act of adultery, the adventure at sea, the flight down the Mississippi. If their society had been able to provide them with sufficient social texture—a texture of manners compressed between the stratifications of class—they would undoubtedly exist more completely within and for themselves, and the dramatic event would impose itself upon us not in the moment of violence, the breach of suspense, or the revelation of sin, but in the gradual penetration of what Mr. Trilling calls "the illusion that snobbery generates," the gradual penetration, this is to say, of the structures of hypocrisy and self-deceit, of pride and venality, which, in a complex, developed society, provide some of the counters against which the creation of true character in fiction becomes possible. The absence of such a society in America, and the consequent moral isolation of the individual, is presumably one of the things *Huckleberry Finn* is about. That is the source of the tension and irony one feels in the relationship between Huck and Jim floating on their raft in the middle of the river and the life passing by them on the shore. The social world of the raft is made up of the niceties, kindnesses, little rituals of comradeship—the manners, if you like—which the boy and the man are able to invent and, with no small difficulty, to maintain as they go along. It is an inadequate world and, at times, an inadequate comradeship. But the world of the shore is worse, for it offers only instances of raw violence, the dramatic substitute in American life and the American novel for a culture's full "hum and buzz of implication," which, if it had been present in the background of *Huckleberry Finn,* would unquestionably have enriched the contrast between the two worlds. As it stands, the novel is impoverished by the simplicity of that contrast, by the necessary thinness of the implication of violence in a culture where violence not merely substitutes for but very largely *is* the "hum and buzz." In much the same way, a great many of the heroes of American fiction appear to us thin and self-enclosed and suffering in a vacuum, for, while we feel the pain of their isolation most acutely and appreciate the anguished lyricism which their pain frequently inspires in them, we almost never see precisely what it is they feel so painfully isolated *from*. This, I think, bothers one even in Mr. Schwartz's *Walden*, which really isn't, as he insists, about society at all. It is about a solitary individual rationalizing his isolation from society. Society itself is nowhere to be found. We have always to take Mr. Thoreau's word that it exists, just as we have always to take Mr. Sherwood Anderson's word and Mr. Thomas Wolfe's word and even, oddly enough, Mr. John Dos Passos' word, and that is never enough. As for Mr. Schwartz's Henry James, it is simply not true that he was not interested in nineteenth-century America. He was, on the contrary, very much interested in it, and his novels are full of it, although the America to be found in them is naturally not the one that interested Mark Twain. James had to discover his America in the form that would make it accessible to his particular kind of sensibility, and that was in the form of a vestigial social class in which the decay of a great mercantile culture had left behind the proprieties, if not the substance, of human conduct, the scarcely observable manners "refined," as Eliot said, "beyond the point of civilization" out of which the tenuous felt life of his novels is compounded. If James had failed to find such a form, we should presumably have been left with nothing but the magnificent sensibilities of his characters floating like ectoplasm about their drawing rooms, and that too would never have been enough.

A great deal of the misunderstanding which these questions of Mr. Schwartz's reveal—at least that part of the misunderstanding which is not deliberate and strategic—would probably have been avoided if he had troubled to take into account Mr. Trilling's more considered discussion of manners in the later essay "Art and Fortune." If, however, he had taken it into account, he would have deprived himself of an argument altogether, for in that essay Mr. Trilling makes it clear to those who, like Mr. Schwartz, read "Manners, Morals, and the Novel" superficially or in purely political terms that he is not interested in "establishing a new genteel tradition in criticism and fiction," although he fully understands that, "where misunderstanding serves others as an advantage, one is helpless to make oneself understood." What he *is* interested in is the relation between the value preoccupations of a culture, especially as they take the form of money and class, and the dramatic meaning which these preoccupations tend to take on in the fiction which a culture produces. If, as he said in "Manners, Morals, and the Novel," the primary work of the novel is "the investigation of reality and illusion," specifically, the penetration of the "illusion that snobbery generates" and if the novel, in dealing with the questions of reality and illusion which are raised by the ideas of money and class, characteristically relies, indeed must rely, upon "an exhaustive exploitation of manners," then we must come at the concept of manners from the standpoint of esthetics and rule Mr. Schwartz's approach entirely out of order.

The esthetic implications of Mr. Trilling's view of manners begin to assert themselves in the section of "Art and Fortune" having to do with the question that so disturbed Mr. Schwartz, the question of "substantiality" in its relation to the thinness of social texture in the American novel. Mr. Trilling said in "Manners, Morals, and the Novel" that "the novel in America diverges from its classical intention, which . . . is the investigation of the problem of reality beginning in the social field." He then went on to say that Henry James was "alone [in the American nineteenth century] in knowing that to scale the moral and esthetic heights in the novel one had to use the ladder of social observation," and he paraphrased the passage in James's life of Hawthorne in which James

> . . . enumerates the things which are lacking to give the American novel the thick social texture of the English novel—no state; barely a specific national name; no sovereign; no court; no aristocracy; no church; no clergy; no army; no diplomatic service; no country gentlemen; no palaces; no castles; no manors; no old country houses; no parsonages; no thatched cottages; no ivied ruins; no cathedrals; no great universities; no public schools; no political society; no sporting class—no Epsom, no Ascot! That is, no sufficiency of means for the display of a variety of manners, no opportunity for the novelist to do his job of searching out reality, not enough complication of appearance to make the job interesting.

In the section on "substantiality" in "Art and Fortune"—passages of which I quoted earlier—Mr. Trilling completes this observation:

> I think that if American novels of the past, whatever their merits of intensity and beauty, have given us very few substantial or memorable people, this is because one of the things which makes for substantiality of character in the novel is precisely the notation of

manners, that is to say, of class traits modified by personality [or, he might have said, personality modified by class traits]. It is impossible to imagine a Silas Wegg or a Smerdyakov or a Félicité (of *A Simple Heart*) or a Mrs. Proudie without the full documentation of their behavior in relation to their own classes and to other classes. All great characters of American fiction, such, say, as Captain Ahab and Natty Bumpo, tend to be mythic because of the rare fineness and abstractness of the ideas they represent; and their very freedom from class gives them a large and glowing generality; for what I have called *substantiality* is not the only quality that makes a character great. They are few in number and special in kind; and American fiction has nothing to show like the huge, swarming, substantial population of the European novel, the substantiality of which is precisely a product of a class existence. In fiction, as perhaps in life, the conscious realization of social class, which is an idea of great power and complexity, easily and quickly produces intention, passion, thought, and what I am calling substantiality. The diminution of the reality of class, however socially desirable in many respects, seems to have the practical effect of diminishing our ability to see people in their difference and specialness.

I take it that no theory of the development of the novel pretending to seriousness or any just estimate of the situation now obtaining for the novel in America can safely be put forward without due allowance for the truth of these observations of Mr. Trilling's. The idea of "substantiality" must cause us to explore in a new and vastly more complicated way the old question of how character shows forth to us from the page of fiction, in what terms exactly do we see that it is *there,* as well as the equally old and still more complicated question of just what *has* happened to character in the course of the novel's development, especially when we remember that it was once so unmistakably *there,* surrounded and enclosed by its world of physical sensation and material form, and remember too that our sense of this world, its thickness and dramatic tone, grew out of the relation that literally existed in the social world of the novel's jurisdiction between character and those elements of being—of class, property, money, and birth—in which it found extensions and violations of itself. We remember the great, roomy world of Fielding and Smollett, Thackeray and Dickens, so crowded with variegated life, so thickly populated with personality, and it is like the world the neurotic knew before trauma put blinders on his psyche; while the novel since Dickens shows a deepening trauma and a progressive dislocation of character from its place in the social scene, with society tending to devolve into abstract social force and then into social change and finally into social injustice, with character thinning down into personality and then into sensibility and finally into nothingness, and with the novel itself moving, as Mark Schorer said, "more and more . . . toward the extremities of poetry and history . . . as the individual finds an ever diminishing social authority with which to identify himself," and experiences increasingly that dropping away of connection between his internal nature and the forms of his social existence, which is the feature of our modern neurotic state.

In Jane Austen one finds the dramatic consequences of this connection displaying themselves in a very pure form, almost at times in the very pure form of social stultification. In the world of her novels gentility is a condition of property. It is a virtue which the inherited possession of land makes mandatory; hence, in the landed it is not one of the attributes in terms of which character is made manifest, for, like certain kinds of respectability in society at large, it is simply something one comes into along with the ancestral estate, without moral effort or conscious application of the will. It nonetheless comprises the etiquette or convention, the standard of what is reasonably predictable or acceptable, in relation to which character, when it is aroused either to act or to will, is shown forth and dramatized. Bad behavior in a gentleman of property comes to us, for example, in the dramatic contrast between what he does and what he is expected to do, and it is in the degree of the contrast that we are able to measure his reality as a character. The man without property but possessing great *personal* gentility is dramatized, on the other hand, in the degree of the contrast between what he *is* and what he is expected to be, for within the terms of the equation "property equals gentility," the man without property is expected to be only vulgar. A third and favorite contrast of Miss Austen's, and one that provides the material for a large part of her characteristic irony, is the contrast between the gentility which the landed inherit with their property and the gentility which some of them possess as an ingredient of spirit and which frequently shows up the inherited kind to be no gentility at all. This latter kind is what sets Anne Elliot in *Persuasion* apart from her sisters and accounts in the end both for her success as a person and her success in making an advantageous marriage, while it is her suitor and later her husband Captain Wentworth's possession of the second kind—gentility without property—that supplies the material circumstances in which her success can be effectively realized. The baronet William Elliot is the type of the landed gentleman who behaves badly and whose badness is dramatized in his violation of the inherited decorum which insists that he behave with gentility.

The dramatic movement of the novel might be said to consist of the process by which each of the three characters exceeds or falls short of the standard of quality laid down by the size of his property holdings. William, through treachery, falls far short of his; Anne, through personal gentility, exceeds hers; Wentworth, through gentility of the same kind, manages without property far to exceed his and barely to equal Anne's.

It might also be said that this process is climaxed in each case by the "penetration" of the reality hidden behind Mr. Trilling's "illusion that snobbery generates," the illusion that masks William's treachery, that obscures Wentworth's true prospects, and that causes us in the beginning to underestimate Anne's character. And one penetrates this illusion in the way Mr. Trilling suggests one always penetrates it in the traditional form of the novel—through the author's "exhaustive exploitation of manners . . . of class traits modified" or, in the case of *Persuasion, enhanced* by "personality." One can also see how it is by virtue of their class traits, their moral arrangement on the scale of property, that the characters of *Persuasion* help give the novel "substantiality," for the obligations which property imposes upon them form the standard by which their actions as characters can be measured and dramatically analyzed. Without these obligations there could have been no *Persuasion* because there would have been no problem. Anne would simply have married Wentworth at once over the materialistic objections of Lady Russell—her objections *are* Anne's "persuasion"—and gone off with him into a life of romantic poverty, while William would have had no decorum to betray and no goal in the name of which to betray it.

One can undoubtedly say the same for the lovers in Charlotte Brontë's *Jane Eyre*. What gives the passion of Jane and Rochester its intensity and dramatic authority is the conflict between the obligations of self-respect and virtue imposed upon Jane by her religious and class background and the fierce demands of Rochester's privileged licentiousness as well as of her own newly awakened emotions. Each of the scenes depicting this passion is played out under the accusing eyes of Jane's stern Calvinist God or, literally, under the shadow of sexual guilt cast by Rochester's mad wife locked in the rooms overhead. And it is one of the compelling ironies of the novel that Jane's moral obligations to herself win out in the end over the passion to which they will not allow her to succumb; for in the end the Providence that destroys Rochester's health and sight also makes it possible for Jane to serve him as she wanted all along to serve her God, not as a lover—for which she never really had much talent anyhow—but as a loving attendant, and to be loved in return, not for her qualities of passion, but for her qualities of service. It is Jane who, after all, wins *Rochester* in the end, and on her own terms. "Reader, I married him," she exclaims on the last page, and the note of triumph in her voice should not escape us. *She has* married him, but only after God has obliged her, as it were, by rendering him impotent and enabling her to keep her vow of chastity in a marriage-become-hospital. Interpreted in this way, *Jane Eyre* may be taken as one of the coldest works of feminist polemics ever written; and it may be taken so, at the level of its deepest and most rewarding subtlety, because the moral obligations imposed by religion and class are there to provide the tension and the complexity, as well as the key to the conflict, in which its true meaning resides.

Raskolnikov's situation in *Crime and Punishment* is a very similar case in point. We are able to appreciate the enormity of his crime and to participate in the anguish of his guilt because the crime comes to us in the context of the morality which it violates, just as the guilt comes to us in the context of the morality out of which it derives. It is the material of participation and judgment which the novel provides through the ingredients of character, scene, and sensory language, rather than the material which we bring with us into the novel out of life, that affords us our angle of vision, that enables us to *see* into Raskolnikov and to assess both his crime and the quality of his conscience. As R. P. Blackmur, in speaking of the ingredient of character in this material, has pointed out, Raskolnikov's mother and his sister Dounia "represent the normal conduct from which Raskolnikov departs; they represent the order of society which he tears down and envelops; it is them, their lives, to whom he gives meaning," and, one might add, it is they, along with Svidrigailov and Razumihin, in their different and opposite ways, who give meaning to *his* life, who by turns estimate and objectify the quality of his conscience.

All that I have been discussing up to now has had to do with the question of the availability of this "order of society," particularly for the novel of the past, and with the related question of the kinds of material—money, property, class, religious scruple—of which, from time to time in the novel, this order may be seen to consist. But it is time now to narrow the focus, to produce *exempla* out of familiar works which will more concretely illustrate just how these materials function, even within single scenes, to help make possible the dramatic delineation of character in fiction, particularly to help produce those instances of tension, discord, and even, at times, of outrage as well as those instances of contrast between appearance and truth, illusion and reality, in which the fullness of character is most often shown forth. I have chosen, more or less at random, two traveling scenes, both, as it happens, coming at the beginning of novels, one from Dostoevski's *The Idiot* and the other from Ford Madox Ford's *Some Do Not,* and as a final example, the "Red Shoes" scene from Proust's *The Guermantes Way*. The fact that the first two are traveling scenes in a sense makes the job harder, for to the novelist the placing and motivating of character presented during travel is very nearly a "whole-cloth" proposition. He is denied access to the customary props of landscape and weather, on the one hand, and of native domestic surroundings and the individualizing habits and routines of daily life on the other, and so is forced to build character entire, really to *see* his Mrs. Brown, as Virginia Woolf would have said, without the help of the crowded Edwardian context which might otherwise have done nearly all his seeing for him. He is, in fact, required to make do—as these scenes show—only with such individualizing effects as may be registered through speech, gesture, and dress and the systems of value and belief which these may represent. In societies and ages in which speech and dress tend to be standardized and in which the prevailing system of value dictates conformity or a promiscuous and therefore a meaningless geniality, one supposes that the scene of travel in fiction would eventually disappear altogether, simply on the ground that there would be little or nothing in the experience of such a scene worth recording; in fact, if we now live in this kind of society and age and can accept some of our current novels as accurately reflecting the reality around us, it would seem that the only experiences now worth recording are those that transpire in psychiatric sanitaria, in the death cells of prisons, in the dim minds of infants, and in bed.

The Idiot opens on a note of incongruity, a situation of contrast between illusion and truth, in which our senses are at once caught up, momentarily deranged, and then set straight. Traveling in a third-class carriage of the Warsaw train now approaching Petersburg are two young men who *appear* to be poor but who begin almost immediately to pull away and move above their shabbiness of dress and their third-class accommodations as the narrative focus clears and as we are allowed to take note of certain as yet unassessable attributes of feature which seem to suggest that they are in some way distinctive as persons.

> One of them was a short man about twenty-seven, with almost black curly hair and small, grey, fiery eyes. He had a broad and flat nose and high cheek bones. His thin lips were continually curved in an insolent, mocking and even malicious smile. But the high and well-shaped forehead redeemed the ignoble lines of the lower part of the face. What was particularly striking about the young man's face was its death-like pallor, which gave him a look of exhaustion in spite of his sturdy figure, and at the same time an almost painfully passionate expression, out of keeping with his coarse and insolent smile and the hard and conceited look in his eyes. . . . [The other] was a young man, also twenty-six or twenty-seven years old, above the average in height, with very fair thick hair, with sunken cheeks and a thin, pointed, almost white beard. His eyes were large, blue and dreamy; there was something gentle, though heavy-looking in their expression, something of that strange look

from which some people can recognize at the first glance a victim of epilepsy. Yet the young man's face was pleasing, thin and clean-cut, though colourless, and at this moment blue with cold.

These descriptions represent the second phase of the developing contrast by means of which the two young men are in the process of being gradually individualized as characters. Seen initially within the stereotype of third-class status and poverty, which leads us to expect them to be mediocre, they are now seen as personally distinctive and, therefore, as personally superior to that stereotype. Then in the next few moments, as conversation between them begins, they declare their identities, and the contrast moves into a third phase: personal distinction within the appearance of poverty is reinforced by actual distinction of class coupled with actual poverty. Or, to put the matter differently, we have been led first to infer from their circumstances that the young men are mediocre; then they are described as having some personal worth even though they are poor. Now we are led to infer from the fact of their aristocratic heritage that they must also have the high social and material status which normally accompanies it, but that is proven wrong by the fact of their poverty. The blond young man is a *Prince* Myshkin, but he is the last of the Prince Myshkins and quite out of pocket. The dark young man, Parfyon Rogozhin, is technically heir to a fortune of two and a half million roubles—one recalls Mr. Trilling's comment that "every situation in Dostoevski, no matter how spiritual, starts with a point of social pride and a certain number of roubles"—but Rogozhin has been temporarily cut off by his family in punishment for a foolish indiscretion. As soon as this information is supplied us, the contrast moves into a fourth phase, the phase of its greatest subtlety, and the young men are presented through the remainder of the scene not simply as possessing some personal worth in the midst of impoverished circumstances but as possessing particular and opposite *kinds* of personal worth which are displayed in their respective attitudes toward the fact that they are both *aristocrats* and in impoverished circumstances. Myshkin is the soul of modesty and refinement. He answers Rogozhin's questions readily and frankly, and he is decent to the petty official Lebedyev who constantly intrudes upon the conversation. Rogozhin, on the other hand, is arrogant and fiercely resentful of his present predicament and refuses to speak directly to Lebedyev at any time. It is the sharp contrast in their treatment of Lebedyev which particularly points up the differences in character of the two men, just as it is Lebedyev from whose angle of vision we observe and measure them and their situation. He is, in fact, the moral center around which the others revolve, for as their problem is one of money, status, and, in Rogozhin's case, social pride, so he represents the value system of class snobbery, political opportunism and influence to which, in men of his type, these are generally vulgarized.

Such omniscient gentlemen [says Dostoevski] are to be found pretty often in a certain stratum of society. They know everything. All the restless curiosity and faculties of their minds are irresistibly bent in one direction, no doubt from lack of more important ideas and interests in life, as the critic of today would explain. But the words, "they know everything," must be taken in a rather limited sense: in what department so-and-so serves, who are his friends, what his income is, where he was governor, who his wife is and what dowry she brought him, who are his first cousins and who are his second cousins, and everything of that sort. For the most part these omniscient gentlemen are out at elbow, and receive a salary of seventeen roubles a month. The people of whose lives they know every detail would be at a loss to imagine their motives. Yet many of them get positive consolation out of this knowledge, which amounts to a complete science, and derive from it self-respect and their highest spiritual gratification.

Lebedyev, then, is of the world of quantitative measurement, of possession, connection, position, and power, the world that is always at the back of the novel and that evaluates and approves the character of Rogozhin as it evaluates and condemns—although not in our eyes—the character of Myshkin. It is what Lebedyev *knows* of this world, and there is nothing he does not know, that enables him to express and then to validate our astonishment as the illusion of poverty that surrounds the young men is gradually penetrated and their identity and true status are revealed. It is in terms of this knowledge, furthermore, that he is able to make the ironic and yet accurately qualitative remark about Myshkin's poor bundle of clothing which puts the scene into focus—"Your bundle has some value, anyway, . . . and though one may safely bet there is no gold in it, neither French, German, nor Dutch—one may be sure of that, if only from the gaiters you have got on over your foreign shoes—yet if you can add to your bundle a relation such as Madame Epanchin, the general's lady, the bundle acquires a very different value. . . ." This is the value that gives us our center, our post of observation onto the scene and that provides the snobbery that generates the illusion that Dostoevski penetrates. But if the elements of class and status of which Lebedyev's value is the hypocrisy were not there in the background of the novel and, by extension, in Dostoevski's moral world, there would be nothing to generate the illusion, hence nothing to penetrate, and there would be no way of dramatizing the scene so that we would move gradually downward through the illusion of class to the reality of class to the reality of character within class, which is the reality at the heart of the power and "substantiality" of the scene.

The dramatics, the characterizing factor, of the first scene in Ford's *Some Do Not* presents itself to us not in the *illusion* of class but in the bare fact. From the opening line to the end, class works consistently and simply to distinguish the characters of the scene from one another and then to document their differences.

> The two young men—they were of the English public official class—sat in the perfectly appointed railway carriage. . . . The compartment smelt faintly, hygienically of admirable varnish—the train ran as smoothly—Tietjens remembered thinking—as British gilt-edged securities. It travelled fast; yet had it swayed or jolted over the rail joints, except at the curve before Tonbridge or over the points at Ashford where these eccentricities are expected and allowed for, Macmaster, Tietjens felt certain, would have written to the company. Perhaps he would even have written to the *Times*. . . . Their class administered the world. . . . If they saw a policeman misbehave, railway porters lack civility, an insufficiency of street lamps, defects in public services or in foreign countries, they saw to it, either with nonchalant Balliol voices, or with letters to the *Times* asking in regretful indignation: "Has the British This or That come to *this!*" Or they wrote, in the serious reviews of which so many still survived, articles taking under their care, manners, the Arts, diplomacy, inter-Imperial trade or the personal reputations of deceased statesmen and men of letters. . . . Macmaster, that is to say, would do all that: of himself Tietjens was not so certain.

Here in the two short opening paragraphs of the scene Ford provides us with the broad terms within which Tietjens and Macmaster are to be dramatized and contrasted. We learn exactly what, for members of the "English public official class," is customary and acceptable; therefore, we know precisely where to place, and how to assess, the two young men in relation to their type. Tietjens begins at once to pull away from the type and to set himself in opposition to it. "The train ran as smoothly—*Tietjens* remembered thinking—as British gilt-edged securities. . . . *Macmaster,* that is to say, would do all that: of himself Tietjens was not so certain." Macmaster, on the other hand, begins by being characterized *within* the type and then, because of the very strenuousness of his conformity to it, he gradually takes on particularity of character. The initial or typical contrast between the two men is shown at the outset in the difference of their physical appearance. Macmaster is

> . . . smallish, Whig; with a trimmed, pointed black beard, such as a smallish man might wear to enhance his already germinated distinction; black hair of a stubborn fibre, drilled down with hard metal brushes; a sharp nose; strong, level teeth; a white, butterfly collar of the smoothness of porcelain; a tie confined by a gold ring, steel-blue speckled with black—to match his eyes, as Tietjens knew. Tietjens, on the other hand, could not remember what coloured tie he had on.

And, as it turns out, Tietjens does not need to remember or to care. Because of his secure position in his class, he can afford the luxury of personal untidiness just as he can afford the luxury of independence in thought and manner. But Macmaster is Scottish and of rather humble origin, and so must conform to the rules of class, must, in fact, continually exert himself to go the rules one better. It is as much the degree of his overtypicalness as it is the degree of Tietjen's undertypicalness that causes him to take on character; but we are able to see and to appreciate that character, and therefore to respond to the dramatics of the scene as a whole, only because we have before us, in the form of Ford's generic description, the pattern of decorum or manners which, in each case, character violates.

The "Red Shoes" scene from *The Guermantes Way* opens with the Duchesse de Guermantes inquiring of Swann whether he will be going to Italy with her and her husband in ten months' time. Swann replies that it will not be possible, that in ten months he will probably already have been dead for several months. Hearing this news while on her way to the carriage which is to take her and the Duke to dinner, the Duchesse stops in confusion.

Placed for the first time in her life between two duties as incompatible as getting into her carriage and shewing pity for a man who was about to die, she could find nothing in the code of conventions that indicated the right line to follow, and not knowing which to choose, felt it better to make a show of not believing that the alternatives need be seriously considered, so as to follow the first, which demanded of her at the moment less effort, and thought that the best way of settling the conflict would be to deny that any existed. "You're joking," she said to Swann. "It would be a joke in charming taste," replied he, ironically. "I don't know why I am telling you this; I have never said a word to you before about my illness. But as you asked me, and as I may die now at any moment. . . . But whatever I do I mustn't make you late; you're dining out, remember," he added, because he knew that for other people their own social obligations took precedence of the death of a friend and could put himself in her place by dint of his instinctive politeness. But that of the Duchesse enabled her to perceive in a vague way that the dinner to which she was going must count for less to Swann than his own death. And so, while continuing on her way to the carriage, she let her shoulders droop saying: "Don't worry about our dinner. It's not of any importance!"

The Duke has heard Swann's news, but his first concern is punctuality, and he urges his wife to hurry. But just as she is entering the carriage, he notices that she is still wearing her black shoes and demands that she change at once into her red ones. The Duchesse returns dutifully to her room, and the Duke asks Swann to leave before she comes down again and delays their departure further by resuming the conversation. The Duke explains that she is tired out already and "will reach the dinner-table quite dead" and that he too is dying of hunger.

"I had a wretched lunch this morning when I came from the train. There was the devil of a *béarnaise* sauce, I admit, but in spite of that I shan't be at all sorry, not at all sorry to sit down to dinner. Five minutes to eight! Oh, women, women! She'll give us both indigestion before tomorrow. She is not nearly as strong as people think." The Duke felt no compunction at speaking thus of his wife's ailments and his own to a dying man, for the former interested him more, appeared to him more important. And so it was simply from good breeding and good fellowship that, after politely shewing us out, he cried "from off stage," in a stentorian voice from the porch to Swann, who was already in the courtyard: "You, now, don't let yourself be taken in by the doctors' nonsense, damn them. They are donkeys. You're as strong as the Pont Neuf. You'll live to bury us all!"

What is most striking about this scene is the extent to which the code of manners of the Duke and Duchesse makes possible their bad behavior to Swann, dictates it, in fact, and makes it acceptable. It is because of their allegiance to convention that they can be dramatized as unfeeling, that we are able to measure the distance between what they ought to do and what they feel they *must* do or cannot help but do. Convention is the point from which, in estimating the scene, we depart. Humanity is the point at which we arrive and they do not, and that is the disparity which gives us our superior knowledge and they their superior force of character. The Duchesse,

> . . . placed for the first time in her life between two duties as incompatible as getting into her carriage and shewing pity for a man who was about to die, . . . could find nothing in the code of conventions that indicated the right line to follow, and not knowing which to choose, felt it better to make a show of not believing that the alternatives need be seriously considered, so as to follow the first, which demanded of her at the moment less effort, and thought that the best way of settling the conflict would be to deny that any existed.

. . . *so as to follow the first,* the alternative of getting into her carriage, the one alternative her code of conventions holds open to her. That is Proust's comment on the grave limitations of that code in his society, and that is the stroke of inhumanity, of bad manners which enlightens the scene for us. We *see* the Duchesse in her decision to renounce the show of pity and to enter her carriage. Her decision, for better or worse, *is* her characterization. If her code dictated a show of pity, we should have humanity but no irony, for the irony comes to us in the contrast between the dictates of true humanity and the dictates of a code which, while ostensibly designed to make true humanity continuously possible, ends by making life frequently cruel. The Duke's parting remark to Swann is given force by a variation of the same contrast. It comes, first of all, as the result of an afterthought, "simply from good breeding and good fellowship," a momentary acknowledgment of a higher etiquette than that of the code. But we already know that "his wife's ailments and his own . . . interested [the Duke] more, appeared to him more important . . . [than] a dying man," and so we are in a position to assess the hypocrisy of the remark and, through it, the hypocrisy of the man. The code of conventions or manners in the scene may be said, therefore, to constitute its binding and compulsive force out of which, when it is violated or when there is brought up against it a more transcendent necessity, conflict and drama are generated.

One is struck by how progressively rarer this has become in the novel with the passage of time, how, for example, in the more purely existentialist fiction of our own day as well as in the typical American novel of tradition, the heroes appear to suffer their guilt in a vacuum or even to suffer nothing which we can rightly call guilt, but only remorse or only self-hatred or, most often lately, only a kind of numbness and vacuity. Even Flaubert's Emma Bovary is partly vitiated as a character because, although the provincial towns in which she lives provide her with a motive for perfidy, they do not provide the active terms in which her perfidy is judged and condemned. It is significant that in a novel dealing with the favorite subject of gossip there should be no gossip, but only the barest peripheral intimation of it, the faintest whispering in the wings. Emma's world is simply not alive enough or concerned enough with life to be able to rouse itself to the task of malice. It is a dull, stupid, complacent world, a world of puff and pomp and provincial oratory, the world of the Homaises, the Rodolphes, and the Charleses. This is one of the reasons Emma despises it so and becomes perfidious, but this is also one of the reasons she is not so solid on the page as we would like. To be driven to do what she does she has to live in an impoverished world, but to be able to evaluate what she is driven to do we have to see her world as something other than impoverished. The same paradox perhaps accounts for Flaubert's failure with Charles, for Charles has to do for the novel what the towns cannot. He has to "represent the normal conduct from which [Emma] departs, . . . the order of society which [she] tears down and envelops," but the difficulty is that the normal conduct is conduct at a minimum, the near refusal to act which is the dullness of respectability; so Charles is required to be both dramatically present as a character and representative of a way of life which is not only undramatic but scarcely present at all; and this he cannot be or, at any rate, this Flaubert cannot make him be convincingly.

In our own novel in recent times there have been at least two instances of writers who have escaped the Bovarist vacuum by virtue of their commitment to social situations in which, for reasons of cultural lag or entrenched religiosity, a moral atmosphere or background remains accessible against which conduct may be posed in a dramatic way. Faulkner in the South works with an atmosphere so charged with guilt and aberration, a background so rich in natural complexity and violence, that it morally burdens his characters almost to excess, keeping them perpetually in a state of hyperesthesia and their conduct perpetually at the brink of melodrama. James T. Farrell, whose *Studs Lonigan* Mr. Trilling has singled out as belonging to that group of novels in which a "concern with manners is of their very essence," achieved a similar, though less spectacular, effect in his early work by exploiting the atmosphere of Shanty Irish piety and hypocrisy in which he grew up, the atmosphere which, through its ironic contrast with the situation of poverty that generates it, affords us the terms of moral measurement for Studs Lonigan's gradual deterioration and for Danny O'Neill's equally gradual redemption. It is interesting to see, however, that while Studs's deterioration is in the strictest keeping with the logic which the poverty imposes, Danny's redemption runs counter to it and forces Farrell to attribute to him qualities of character which cannot be objectified through the naturalistic method and which, therefore, seem to us excessive and inexplicable. The only *dramatic* qualities of aspiration and transcendence which the O'Neill novels do contain, furthermore, are those framed in the context of piety and hypocrisy, which means that when we cast about for a justification for Danny's redemption, we cannot help but find it in that context and assume that he too is pious and hypocritical.

Mr. Morton Dauwen Zabel, in his excellent short study of Graham Greene, could well have been thinking of Danny's problem along with the problem of what I have been calling the "Bovarist vacuum" when he said:

> A criminal takes his dignity from his defiance of the intelligence or merit that surrounds him, from the test his act imposes on the human community. He becomes trivial when that measure is denied him. . . . The hardship this imposes on the artist is obvious. When felony, by becoming political, becomes impersonal; when the *acte gratuit* elicits not only secret but public approval, its dramatist faces

the desperate task of restoring to his readers their lost instinct of values, the sense of human worth. . . . The Victorian *frisson* of crime was all the choicer for the rigor of propriety and sentiment that hedged it in. Dickens's terrors are enhanced less by his rhetoric than by his coziness. The reversion to criminality in Dostoevski takes place in a ramifying hierarchy of authority—family life, social caste, political and religious bureaucracy, czarist militarism and repression. The horror of "The Turn of the Screw" is framed by the severest decorum, taste, and inhibition.

And finally Mr. Zabel has said:

Where once—in James, Conrad, Dostoevski, in Dickens, Defoe, and the Elizabethans—it was society, state, kingdom, world, or the universe itself that supplied the presiding order of law or justice, it is now the isolated, betrayed, and finally indestructible integrity of the individual life that must furnish that measure. Humanity, having contrived a world of mindless and psychotic brutality, reverts for survival to the atom of the single man. Marked, hunted, Ishmaelite, or condemned, he may work for evil or for good, but it is his passion for a moral identity of his own that provides the nexus of values in a world that has reverted to anarchy.

It is in relation to a world of somewhat near this kind, in which by now I take it we all more or less recognize we live or have lived, that the problem of the "Bovarist vacuum" in fiction may be seen in its widest significance. This is to say that to see it best we must come at it not by beginning with Flaubert but by beginning now, with all that we know in our present moment of history, and moving back on Flaubert reflexively through the vast and discouraging stretches of the post-Flaubertian experience. But to perceive this world we must have lived with the perception in our bones, not as a fact of knowledge but as a fact of sense, and have retained a view of fiction, at least of everything in fiction that may be said to be *given,* up to and perhaps even beyond the instant genius begins its work, as the gauge of morals and morale of the world out of which it comes. By gauge I do not mean Stendhal's "mirror dawdling down a lane" or the literary counterpart of a photograph by Cartier-Bresson. I mean an instrument whose function it is to translate into its own system of measurement and its own scale of relationships the impressions that come in upon it from a reality of which the impressions are necessarily measured and related according to a different system and scale, or are not measured or related at all.

John Peale Bishop perhaps had in mind some such idea of fiction as this when he said, "It is the mark of the true novelist that in searching the meaning of his own unsought experience, he comes on the moral history of his time." Certainly, it is the "unsought experience" merely that the average fiction of a time is most likely to give us, unsought by the novelist and unwelcomed by us. And it is the "moral history" that we always want when we can get it and the novelist can get at it, and when it is there in his time to be got at in a form moral enough to give it a range and significance larger than history.

FOUR

Gray new world

THE IMPACT OF David Riesman's work over the past several years has been such that any general discussion of his ideas at this time must appear superfluous. It may be said with certainty that Riesman, for better or worse, is now in the public domain, and even though his "position" in the more advanced circles of the mind has been under sporadic siege, one cannot help but acknowledge the successes recently made by the hired legions of Time, Inc., in effecting his release into middle-brow adulation. Riesman has now, we may say, begun to suffer the typical fate of the good writer or thinker in America, particularly of the kind in whom talent has joined with a sense of the age to produce a meretriciousness nearly indistinguishable from the glow of prophecy. He has lived to see himself become, at the height of his career, a sort of mythmaker and culture hero of the leisure-oriented educated classes, the same classes which, a generation ago, took up Spengler, Ortega, and Freud, but which tend today not so much to fashion themselves on ideas as passively to consume them, without noticeable decrease of pallor. His key terms have become established as the common coin of the new cocktail-and-breezeway Bohemia—from which, ironically, the concepts behind some of them derive—and they have had bestowed upon them what in this country is the final proof of popular acceptance—the accolade of misquotation by the illiterately well-read. *The Lonely Crowd,* Riesman's core work, is now a best seller in the abridged paper-backed edition; the number of servants its author keeps in his Chicago house has been for several months a matter of public record. At the colleges the brighter students—in contrast to their elders—are forming themselves on his categories, quite consciously seeking "autonomy," and looking ahead to the time when they will be able to take a course in it. Others still brighter are discovering in "other-direction" a patent excuse for their silence and conformism.

Meanwhile, from the intellectualist camp the sniping continues. In the Autumn, 1954, issues of *Partisan Review* and *Dissent* Elizabeth Hardwick and Norman Mailer, reviewing Riesman's latest book, *Individualism Reconsidered* together charge him with a variety of offenses ranging from opportunism through conservatism to complacent optimism about the changing character of our culture. Mailer's discussion, which I take to be the most penetrating we have yet had of Riesman's whole "case," turns on the excellent point that what Riesman has given us is essentially a fiction rather than a sociological analysis of American culture, a creative image whose value must be judged not by its truth to Reality—if such exists—but as in a novel by the quality of the mind, and the depth of the life, behind it. While in Riesman's case Mailer does not assess either of these at very much, his point seems to me an important one in putting us onto the primary fact about the best of Riesman's work, particularly *The Lonely Crowd:* that within its obvious and perhaps very narrow limits, it is wholly successful as a work of the creative and intuitive intelligence. The insights it employs differ in quality but not in kind from the insights employed in any serious novel to achieve realism or verisimilitude, and its success derives like a novel's from the thoroughness with which it explores and dramatizes the problems set by its subject. I imagine that this sort of success, in place of the sterner academic variety, is one of the reasons Riesman has earned such a large share of dislike among critics. Another may be that taken merely as sociology such a book as *The Lonely Crowd* at once runs afoul of our current mistrust of all programmatic definitions and set formulas and our vastly inflated egocentricity, which causes us to reject those definitions which take into account less of life than we are daily bewildered by. But taken as a fiction *The Lonely Crowd* presents us with a dramatic image of ourselves which we can respond to and learn from, just as we can learn from the image of ourselves thrown back by the caricaturing fun-house mirror of a first-rate novel of manners. It does not matter that the image is not "true" and does not do us justice. Neither are statistics and graphs "true," and certainly they never do us justice. What matters is that the image has its own justice and that its very distortion may reflect tendencies in us which in twenty or thirty years will become our truth.

In this sense, I believe *The Lonely Crowd* to be one of the most important literary expressions the present age in America has had, a book to rank in its implications for Western culture with *The Revolt of the Masses* and *Democracy in America.* It is a book, furthermore, which, because it is backed by a creative consciousness of high order, opens for us in a new way the old question of the relationship between literature and society, between the novelist and those portions of his material which we may take to be environmentally given, yet which from novelist to novelist are never seen to be precisely the same. I should like to argue that, in addition to its relevance to us all, *The Lonely Crowd* is a book which no novelist at the present time can safely ignore or wholly escape, for it may be read as a record of the disappearance from our culture of the social forms which have traditionally afforded the novel its dramatic materials.

What Riesman calls the "inner-directed" man has been the typical hero of fiction from its beginnings and of drama from antiquity. Whether we begin with Oedipus and Tom Jones or Odysseus and Don Quixote, we find the recurring source of drama in the conflict between the obsessive inner drives of the hero and the moral structures of his society which work to deny them fulfillment. One can in fact say that as the novel has evolved, its form has tended to imitate the movement of the "inner-directed" hero through the various phases of this conflict, as the curve of classical tragedy with its culminating recognition-reversal effect represents the archetypal imitation.

The "investigation of illusion and reality," which Lionel Trilling considers to be the proper business of the novel, quite literally depends upon the existence of some "inner-directed" ideal or dream that is so compulsive and blinding in its force that it causes the hero not to *see* or to refuse to *see* in time. Then, as a rule, the novel transports him, and us with him, through a body of experience which proves his illusion to *be* illusion and reality, as always, to be transcendent. When this proof appears, we have our moment of recognition and, nearly always, our moment of purgation, for the hero has by now clearly failed, fallen short, been duped, and so must go down in defeat. Or he has undergone initiation, conversion, and been reborn phoenixlike out of the ashes of his former self.

From the Greeks down, indeed, from Venus and Adonis and the early fertility cults down, we acknowledge this to be the pattern of our racial inheritance; it is in fact the pattern through which our minds naturally express our sense of the cycle and rhythm of life itself; and we recognize its recurrence again and again in the drama, the story, and the novel. It has given us in modern times some of our most memorable fictional characters—Emma Bovary, Lambert Strether, Raskolnikov, Babbitt, Axel Heyst, Jay Gatsby, Frederic Henry, Willie Stark, Willy Loman—and in the novel of the past, where it tends to be clearer because more firmly buttressed by the dramatizing agents of property, religion, money, and class, it has given us very nearly the whole of our formula for seeing and evaluating the reality around us. So completely has this been true that it is only with the greatest difficulty, the most painful renovation of our habits of insight, that we can discard its stereotype and see in the new reality around us the change which has rendered the stereotype invalid.

This change which, if Riesman is correct, has resulted in the rise of a new "other-directed" personality type, must cause us drastically to revise our conception of drama, just as it must drive the novel either to extinction or to the discovery of new dramatic effects. With the disappearance of "inner-directed" man the illusion generated by ideals also disappears, along with the dramatic action taken in the name of ideals, and drama of the traditional kind becomes impossible. What the new "other-directed" man apparently requires is the approval of others, usually of the others in what Riesman calls his "peer-group." But the difficulty from the standpoint of drama is that the need for approval does not express itself in the form of an ideal nor represent a basis for dramatic action. It is not a drive compelling the individual toward the realization of selfhood. It seems, in fact, to have no ideological basis whatever, but is simply the result of a vague, generalized feeling of anxiety. The need to please others does have, however, a very real though largely unrecognized practical basis. In a society in which, as Riesman shows, "inner-directed" traits are no longer required by industry and, therefore, no longer serve as criteria for the judgment of individual worth, a person's agreeableness or niceness becomes one of the main criteria by which he can be judged; his "personality" becomes his distinguishing or salable commodity. But "personality" in such a society does not mean a set of traits which particularize or set off an individual from others. The requirement that he be approved of by everyone forces the individual, on the contrary, to suppress his particularizing traits—if he has any—on the ground that someone, anyone, might not like them, with the result that "personality" becomes, for him, innocuousness and anonymity. What we are therefore faced with in Riesman's gray new world is a situation in which the drives have disappeared which might have caused the individual to act dramatically and, at the same time, a situation in which dramatic action is seen as a threat to the one kind of satisfaction which the society still considers worthwhile.

We ought also to take into account the parallel disappearance in Riesman's world of the older patterns of social class as our way of life has become increasingly standardized, as wealth has come to be distributed more widely and evenly, and as aristocratic traditions have grown thin. One effect of this has been to deprive the novelist of the means of distinguishing among characters through differences in their appearance and manners, social position, and breeding. He has also been deprived of some of his oldest themes—the movement of the individual up and down the scale of class; his struggle for wealth and prestige; his moral orientation toward money, money not simply to buy *things* but to keep up the family honor or estate, as one sees it dramatized in Jane Austen, George Eliot, and Henry James; and lastly what Lionel Trilling has called the theme of the "Young Man from the Provinces." This is the young man of "provincial birth and rearing . . . [who] starts with a great demand upon life and a great wonder about its complexity and promise. He may be of good family but he must be poor. He is intelligent . . . but not at all shrewd in worldly matters. He must have acquired a certain amount of education, should have learned something about life from books, although not the truth." He should be in a position to move from a state of innocence to a state of knowledge, from "inner-directed" idealism, perhaps, to initiation in "other-directed" experience. Mr. Trilling mentions several novels in which the Young Man from the Provinces has figured as hero—*The Red and the Black, Père Goriot* and *Lost Illusions, Great Expectations, Sentimental Education,* perhaps *War and Peace* and *The Idiot.* And one can add to the list out of our own literature perhaps *The Leatherstocking Tales, Huckleberry Finn, The Red Badge of Courage,* some of James, *An American Tragedy,* some of Lewis, *Winesburg, Ohio* and *Dark Laughter, In Our Time, One Man's Initiation, Manhattan Transfer,* parts of *USA,* all of Fitzgerald and Wolfe, *The Wild Palms,* Farrell's Studs Lonigan and Danny O'Neill novels, and coming up to the present, *All the King's Men, Catcher in the Rye, Other Voices, Other Rooms, End as a Man, The Heart Is a Lonely Hunter,* and *The Adventures of Augie March.*

The novelist in the predominantly "other-directed" culture of today, however, is faced with a situation in which increasingly everyone tends to look, dress, and act like everyone else, to drive the same cars, to live in the same kind of houses, and, because of the power of the mass media, even to think the same thoughts. As for the Young Man from the Provinces, he is an antique figure, a literary stereotype of which the type in life can scarcely be said any longer to exist. The ignorant, domineering parents and community which he characteristically rejected in the name of his ideal, his illusion of life as it should be, have been replaced, for the most part, by parents of intelligence and understanding, and by a community which so closely resembles the city to which he formerly escaped that there is no effective difference between them. The Young Man himself, or his comparable type, is no longer provincial or idealistic. Dreams of glory, wealth, and adventure no longer obsess him. His future course is clear and realistic. The safe job with the corporation or university, the pretty wife and children, the prefabricated ranch-style house with the picture window, rumpus room, and breezeway, the Ford that looks like a Cadillac—these are the goals toward which his heroism is directed, his dramatic escape is made.

The movement which, in the last fifty years, the novel in America records is the movement gradually away from the "inner-directed" phase of our cultural development toward the phase of at least incipient "other-direction." In Dreiser, Lewis, Fitzgerald, Dos Passos, Wolfe, and Farrell one is repeatedly struck by how much the dramatic intensity depends upon the conflict between the rural and pioneer virtues of moral innocence, honesty, thrift, and fidelity, on the one hand, and the urban and modern attributes of knowledge, corruption, infidelity, and promiscuity on the other. One also recognizes just as often the conflict between the provincial drives toward material success and increased social status and the resistance put up against them by competition or prejudice or political chicanery. Lewis's Babbitt is what might be called an "inner-directed, other-directed" type. Like the "other directed" business man of today, Babbitt wants to be well liked, but the vastly important distinction to be made between the two is that Babbitt has strongly "inner-directed" reasons for wanting to be well liked. He wants success, wealth, and position; while today's business man usually wants merely security and, in his lonely isolation from the motives and springs of being, a constant assurance that he is accepted by others. Fitzgerald's Gatsby is a perfect example of the strongly "inner-directed" type dedicated to the fulfillment of his dream in a society already passing into "other-direction." Nick Carraway, furthermore, is the type of the provincial Young Man who, in the face of the corruption of this society, does Gatsby's learning for him, conducts his moral education by proxy. Jack Burden functions in Warren's *All the King's Men* in a very similar way. Willie Stark, the fiercely "inner-directed" man, dies unchanged and essentially undefeated, but Jack is initiated and undergoes conversion, is metaphorically reborn with a new father and mother, a new past and future, a future based largely on the virtues of "other-direction." The heroes of Farrell and Wolfe are nearly all drawn on the type of the provincial Young Man. Eugene Gant, George Webber, Studs Lonigan, and Danny O'Neill are simply confronted with experience, most of it for the first time, and the novels record their reactions, their progress toward moral fulfillment or destruction.

When we come to the thirties, however, we notice that the novels depicting the change from "inner-" to "other-direction" begin to be replaced by novels in which social scene gives way to social crisis and the portrayal of special social groups victimized by the Depression. Farrell's work overlaps this category, and the novels of Steinbeck and Caldwell are centered directly within it. Through the novels of the forties and World War II the social scene recedes still further, the Depression disappears, and there develops a preoccupation with social and psychological *problems*—the war experience, race prejudice, homosexuality, and insanity. Now in the fifties these subjects have largely faded out; the social scene is scarcely discernible; and there are signs in the novel of concentration upon rather thin childhood and domestic situations, in which the drama tends to center in a subtle psychic conflict between characters and in which occasionally a climaxing instance of violence effects in them a species of conversion—as happens in Jean Stafford's *The Mountain Lion,* Robie Macauley's *The Disguises of Love,* and Peter Matthiesen's *Race Rock.*

Not only does the reflection of the social scene in novels after the twenties and thirties seem repetitious following the appearance of such books as *The Great Gatsby* and *USA,* but the social scene itself, marked as it is by increasing "other-direction," tends to be less and less *worth* reflecting. It is quite possible, although it may well be brash, to argue that most Americans today literally don't *do* anything. Their goal is, in fact, a condition of life in which they will not be required to do anything ever again. This, I suspect, is what the poet John Berryman meant when he said that "a man can live his whole life in this country without finding out whether or not he is a coward." The novel has consequently been forced to concern itself with more and more marginal and aberrant subjects in its unceasing effort to keep alive and to discover fresh materials for drama. The movement from social manners to social crisis to perversion to the stunted domestic epiphany may be seen in this sense to represent the novel's adjustment to the gradual failure of dramatic possibilities in our culture.

It is perfectly true that the disappearance of "inner-directed" manners has been accompanied by the emergence of "other-directed" manners, and that we are already beginning to experience the effects of the major shift occurring in our social structure, the formation of new patterns of behavior and the rise of new social classes. To take one example alone, one notices how the transferral of power from solitary man and class man to "man among others" has added a new intensity and dimension to our *relations* with others. Where once power and status depended largely upon a man's individual worth, the perfection of his individual talent, or his place in his class, it has now come to depend more and more upon the success of his momentary contacts with persons of influence, on the status which, in their presence, he is able to confer upon himself through his geniality or the breadth of his conversational knowledge in one evening over cocktails. That is probably one of the reasons why we place so much stress on the care and maintenance of our personalities, and why one of the greatest crimes a person can commit today is failure to *appear* to be warm and friendly. In a society where everybody is competent, or competent enough, and nobody really knows what anybody else's true status is, everything depends on the impression one makes with one's personality. That may also be the reason why we have evolved a whole new convention of speech, a convention which allows us to assert ourselves to others provided we *appear* always to be deferring to them, a convention which allows us occasionally even to express an unpopular or disturbing opinion, but always provided we take great care to express it to the accompaniment of the affected stutter or the telltale circling finger—the false symbols of our uncertainty and fallibility, our talismanic assurances to others that we really don't know any more about this than they do, that, after all, we're just average, common people like they are, and, above all else, that we love them just the same. The development which has substituted conversation for communion, contrived geniality for true fellow feeling, and political hospitality for honest friendship is, indeed, a symptom of cultural change. But the question we must ask, the question the novel always asks, is to what end are these new struggles for status directed, by what philosophy or ideal of life are they motivated, and what use does the individual make of this status when he finally gets it? If he does nothing with it but retreat into it and go to sleep, if its gain or loss costs him nothing or changes him in no way, then the novel too must retreat or simply be left by itself to contemplate the depths of its own vacuity.

AUTHOR'S NOTE

SINCE the "Gray New World" essay was written, the novels which implicitly or explicitly affirm the conformist values of the new mass culture have become numerous enough to constitute very nearly a distinct fictional category. Both at the time of its appearance and afterward, Herman Wouk's *The Caine Mutiny* was repeatedly attacked for its conformist propaganda. Of the several critiques Harvey Swados's devastating *Partisan Review* essay was undoubtedly the best, in that it rendered superfluous all further efforts to pin down the causes both of Mr. Wouk's peculiar offensiveness in the novel and his remarkable public popularity—the two being, as Mr. Swados shows, quite obviously identical. The same causes apparently operate to the same ends in the case of *Marjorie Morningstar*. At any rate, one sees Mr. Wouk displaying his familiar and by now thoroughly ritualistic biases. The young intellectual Noel Airman is portrayed with fitting repulsiveness and is made to end his pretentious literary career in deserved third-rate mediocrity. The heroine, after flirting with the gay Bohemian life and paying for it with her virtue, finally settles down to a nice, respectable, motherly middle age in Mamaroneck. But as in *The Caine Mutiny* the popular appeal of *Marjorie Morningstar* does not reside solely, or perhaps even primarily, in such tired and simplified dramatic norms. Whatever one may think of Wouk, one must never underestimate the complexity of the mechanism which has made it possible for him to contact his audience and compel their immediate attention on such a variety of levels of response. As the *Caine Mutiny* audience was allowed to participate vicariously in both defiance of established authority—the relieving of Queeg—and a concluding affirmation of its necessity—the defense of Queeg—so the audience for the new novel is given the initial thrill of vicarious sex and rebellion and the restoring and cleansing palliative of sober respectability. By means of this formula, which one can be certain is unconsciously arrived at, Wouk makes it possible for his readers to drain off their secret frustrations and, at the same time, to think of the draining as harmless since it occurs within the affirming hierarchy of conventional conduct which both Wouk and polite society equally respect. Through his novels they can enjoy the forbidden pleasures of dangerous living and, in the very middle of the act, be assured that pleasureless respectability is the only worthwhile way of life, in short, that they are right to like what they are stuck with. The reverse is true of the majority of modern American novels which, as *Life* editorialists never tire of pointing out, are filled with sex, violence, and corruption, but which disturb the average reader by suggesting that he is somehow living too dull a life or has missed something vital in his past. The great service which Wouk performs for the peace of mind of the American public consists in his attributing to dullness and mediocrity the moral and esthetic virtue which other writers normally reserve for the dedicated and richly imaginative life, and in so doing he has become one of the first American writers to give the public both the courage and the moral obligation to be ordinary.

Still another example of the conformist trend in fiction is Sloan Wilson's *The Man in the Gray Flannel Suit,* a novel which, for the usual reasons, a *Life* editorialist recently found pleasing for its "affirmative" qualities. These qualities are of course obvious throughout the novel and can be held accountable for its popularity. They consist of easy "affirmations" of the status quo, the joys of community service, family life, being happy and contented. But the novel is far more instructive when read as a testimonial of the new American conservative philosophy, the shifts that have lately occurred in our success goals, the drastic changes that have transformed our collective pursuit of the productive life. The novel is, in a very real sense, a thinly fictional portrait of Riesman's gray new world. The hero is caught in a dilemma which fifty years ago would have been inconceivable: he must decide whether to pursue success, power, and wealth at the expense of his personal happiness or to content himself with a small, subordinate job which will allow him to spend time with his family, his house, his front lawn, his car, and his community. The problem is of course not a difficult one nor very long in the solution. In fact, the novel dramatizes the solution before it is fairly under way. The hero's employer is a prototype of the old-fashioned tycoon, left over from the era of economic expansion before dictatorship and paternalism in industry succumbed to fraternalism and manipulation. And the employer is clearly no longer the sort of man one should take one's bearings on. With all his power, wealth, and prestige he is miserably unhappy, estranged from his wife and his daughter, incapable of finding meaning in his life. He is a tragic example to those who would think to aspire and succeed, the perfect witness of the cultural death of Horatio Alger. The only answer for the hero is happy compromise, and when he assents to it, he receives his reward; he *becomes* happy; his wife and children love him once again; he is recognized as a man of importance in his community; he begins to *live*. And so we find ourselves back where we started, in the good old Woukean world. It would be pleasant to be able to detect in it all some dark Republican conspiracy, but there is none. It was merely inevitable at this point in our national development, when we have grown accustomed to having what we want, that we should also produce writers like Wouk and Wilson who are able and willing to sell us what we like to hear.

FIVE

The society of three novels

I ASSUME THAT the questions concerning fiction which most urgently press upon us at this time are these: first, the question of the method by which serious works of fiction show forth their seriousness to us, enable us to recognize them as significant and dramatic, in the degree of their removal from mere lifelikeness; and second, the apparently, but only apparently, contradictory question of the relationship obtaining between the social milieu of serious fiction—the milieu in which the lifelikeness of the unserious usually begins and ends—and the milieu of artifice, implication, ambiguity, paradox, and irony which serious fiction may be said to constitute—the milieu which replaces lifelikeness, life unarranged, with an illusion of life rearranged and invested with order and newly displayed in the terms of significant form. I assume, further, that in seeking an answer to these questions we accept as something given, constant, and essentially impenetrable the factor of talent or genius, and that, therefore, we shall be concerned with only those elements which may be supposed to be available to talent or genius in the world outside the work and to come into fiction only after the operation of talent or genius begins. The problem of the "quality of the mind of the producer," as James put it, is a mysterious one, for we can know that quality only through the quality of the work it accomplishes, and cannot know what minds of quality in any time were unable to accomplish or how much more they might have accomplished had they had the advantage of a more congenial time. But what we can know is the kind of materials which in the past minds of quality seemed typically to need and which they seemed typically to exploit with best results, and we can then apply that knowledge to our own time. Our question, then, will not be the quality of the mind behind the work, but the quality of the world before the mind, and the uses which the mind seems able to make of that world. It is true that the quality of the mind behind the work may still be measured in our own time in the uses to which it can put the world it has before it, but this comes to us most often in one of those forms of damage and distortion, of disparity between content and force, insight and significance, which record all too clearly the consequences of creative power set loose amid paucity and required to make up too strenuously out of its own resources the dramatic materials that ought by rights to be provided by the world before it.

In attempting to formulate an approach to these questions I have selected for analysis three novels of recognized merit published over the last several years. They are J. D. Salinger's *The Catcher in the Rye,* Saul Bellow's *The Adventures of Augie March,* and William Styron's *Lie Down in Darkness.* I have chosen these novels not only because I believe them to be serious and, in their different ways, dramatically significant, but because each has enjoyed a certain notoriety and a certain position of esteem in the popular criticism of the day. It is by now taken for granted that a new novel of discernible merit—it being so rare and remarkable a phenomenon—will automatically be received in the market place with an amount of acclaim greater than it deserves and that a halo of nearly religious luminosity will tend to settle around it, obscuring its real nature in magnification of its virtue, so that it appears in time to exist in a condition of permanent moral elephantiasis. No one, as a rule, feels himself entitled to examine such a work after this ailment sets in—in fear, one supposes, of discovering the ailment to be merely psychogenic in origin—and since we have no higher board of criticism before which the work is required to pass, it usually proceeds on its way to distinction or extinction firmly capsulated and virginal. In the case of these three novels, which have already, at least officially, been sent on their way, I have intended to violate this practice, cut through the luminous halo enclosing them, and see them in a fresh perspective, first, in order to mitigate as much as I can the inflamed judgment imposed upon them by a criticism which is resigned to grading perpetually on the curve, and, second, in order to discover what facts they will yield to help us arrive at an answer to the questions which I raised in the beginning. In choosing these novels specifically, I have been guided, finally, by the assumption that each conceals in its heart more than an ordinary obligation to the society in which we now live, each has to do with problems of value and belief peculiar to this society, and each represents an approach to the problem of dramatizing value and belief through the notation of social manners.

Mr. Salinger's *The Catcher in the Rye,* like *The Adventures of Huckleberry Finn,* is a study in the spiritual picaresque, the journey that for the young is all one way, from holy innocence to such knowledge as the world offers, from the reality which illusion demands and thinks it sees to the illusion which reality insists, at the point of madness, we settle for. But the great difference between the two novels is the measure not merely of the change in time and history of a cultural situation, but of the changed moral circumstances in which innocence typically finds itself in crisis and lends itself to drama. The innocence of *Huckleberry Finn* is a compound of frontier ignorance, juvenile delinquency, and penny-dreadful heroism. It begs for the challenge of thugs, thieves, swindlers, and feuds, and that is what it gets and delights in, takes such delight in, in fact, that even when the dangers become real and the escapes increasingly narrow, we know it is all in fun, that this is innocence living out its concocted daydream of glory in which no one really gets hurt, and even the corpses climb to their feet and dust themselves off at dinnertime. Still, in the suspension of our disbelief, in the planned illusion of the novel itself, the innocence and the world of violence appear to be seriously and effectively opposed. The innocence is the raft to which Huck and Jim, in flight from the dangers of the shore, make their narrow escapes. It is the river itself, time, faith, continuity, moving endlessly and dependably beside and between the temporary and futile altercations of men. And it is the raft and the river together which give the innocence of *Huckleberry Finn* its focus and breadth of implication, so that it exists at once on the level of naïveté at which it responds to adventure and on the level of maturity at which it lends itself to allegory.

The innocence of Mr. Salinger's Holden Caulfield, on the other hand, is a compound of urban intelligence, juvenile contempt, and *New Yorker* sentimentalism, and the only challenge it begs for, the only challenge it has left to beg for, is the challenge of the genuine, the truly human, in a world which has lost both the means of adventure and the means of love. But it is in the nature of Holden's dilemma, his spiritual confinement in this world, that he lacks a concrete basis, can find no concrete embodiment, for the ideal against which he judges, and finds wanting, the life around him. He has objects for his contempt but no objects other than his sister for his love—no raft, no river, no Jim, and no Tom. He is forced, consequently, simply to register his contempt, his developing disillusionment; and it is inevitable that he should seem after a time to be registering it in a vacuum, for just as he can find no concrete equivalent in life for the ideal which he wishes life to embody, so the persons on whom he registers his contempt seem inadequate to it and unjustly accused by it. The boorish prep school roommate, the hypocritical teacher, the stupid women in the Lavender Room, the resentful prostitute, the conventional girl friend, the bewildered cab driver, the affected young man at the theater, the old friend who reveals that his interest in Holden is homosexual—these people are all truly objectionable and deserve the places Holden assigns them in his secret hierarchy of class with its categories of phonies, bores, deceivers, and perverts. But they are nonetheless human, albeit dehumanized, and constitute a fair average of what the culture affords. They are part of the truth which Holden does not see and, as it turns out, is never able to see—that this is what one part of humanity *is;* the lies, the phoniness, the hypocrisy are the compromises which innocence is forced by the world to make. This is the reality on which Holden's illusion is finally broken, but no recognition follows, and no conversion. He remains at the end what he was at the beginning—cynical, defiant, and blind. And as for ourselves, there is identification but no insight, a sense of pathos but not of tragedy. It may be that Mr. Salinger made the most of his subject, but his subject was not adequate to his intention, just as Holden's world is not adequate to his contempt, and that is probably because it does not possess sufficient humanity to make the search for humanity dramatically feasible.

Mr. Saul Bellow's *The Adventures of Augie March* is still another study in the spiritual picaresque, a later form of the traditional *bildungsroman* in which the *pícaro* or hero is consciousness rather than swashbuckling rogue, and so is required, as the rogue is not, to develop, deepen, strike through its first illusion to the truth which, at the end of the road, it discovers to be its fate. But *Augie March* begins with the aphorism, "Man's character is his fate," and it ends with the aphorism transposed "man's fate is his character." The learning is in the transposition. Man's fate is that he shall inherit, be stuck with, his character. The movement which the transposition represents is the movement from the naturalistic to the existentialist, from what is determined to what is accepted or chosen. Augie at the end of the road simply comes into his destiny, although, as it happens, it is not the destiny, the alternative to the "disappointed life," for which he sought. It is the destiny which his character fated, and so, like the rogues of literature in the past, he is not changed but confirmed. I suspect we accept this in those earlier rogues because, having recognized their qualities of character at the outset, we turn our attention to the manner in which these qualities display themselves from adventure to adventure, and find there a confirmation of what we recognized. The emphasis is not on what the hero becomes but on what he does and the bizarreness and excitement of what he does. We know, besides, that his destiny, when it is achieved, will be a formula and a fake—a magical inheritance, a last-minute revelation of noble birth, the conquest of beauty, a "happily ever after." The drama is in the adventure, our interest in being titillated and duped. But the problem which immediately presents itself in the case of Augie is that while his adventures are formed in the pattern of the traditional picaresque, his character demands exposition through the developing form of the more modern *bildungsroman*. He is a Stephen Dedalus set adrift in a world made for Moll Flanders or a Jonathan Wild. As a man with a mission, he is required to impose his will on his experience, to subdue or be subdued, and so to change. But Mr. Bellow feels his obligation to the picaresque too strongly, particularly to the requirement that he who begins as a *pícaro* must end as a *pícaro,* and so we are left at the end with the mission unfulfilled, the will unimposed, the man unsubdued.

To have been an altogether successful adaptation of the picaresque form, the novel would have had to consist of a series of episodes recounting high adventure and intrigue, with an overlay of equally high comedy and social satire. We would then have been placed in the position to appreciate and find full satisfaction in the quality of the adventure and in the confirmation of what we already knew to be Augie's character as he engaged the adventure. But the adventure in the novel as it stands is neither high enough nor rich enough to be a justification of the whole, and we are struck more by Augie's isolation from than by his participation in the social scene of satire. That is, in fact, the necessity which the theme of the novel imposes upon him. He must be disengaged because he must hold out. As the novel develops, we begin to notice, furthermore, as we notice in *Catcher in the Rye,* that the social scene tends to become rarefied and increasingly inspecific. It is not a proper subject for the traditional picaresque satire of the foibles and frailties of class, although the novel does contain many excellent portraits of people. The class structure is simply not there to be satirized, except insofar as the status of individuals is related to money. What one sees is simply the rich and the poor, and these consequently become the poles of commitment between which Augie vacillates. It is interesting to see, however, that the novel in its early sections partakes of some of the dramatic advantages arising out of the racial and economic tensions of lower-class urban experience, a type of experience which in the twenties and thirties was much more common to our larger cities than it is now. The Depression experience alone, in fact, provides Mr. Bellow with nearly all the social and class materials he has, as well as with the perspective of under-privilege from which to judge those materials. But in the early sections we are plunged into a crowded and fully developed world, alive with discord and tensions. There are Augie's mother, his brothers Simon and Georgie, and Grandma Lausch, the Kinsmans, the Coblins, the Kleins, Bluegren and Clem Tambow, the Einhorns, the Commissioner, Kreindl, and Dingbat. But later on, as Augie matures, this world is left behind, the tensions slacken, the social scene becomes depopulated, and we move from a closely interacting mass of people to isolated personalities—the Renlings, the Fenchels, Cissy Flexner, Padilla, Mimi Villars, Hooker Frazer, the Magnuses, then Thea Fenchel, the millionaire Robey, Kayo Obermark, Mintouchian, Basteshaw, and finally Stella. And as this development occurs, the narrative slows and thins out, and Augie's pilgrimage becomes merely a horizontal and unmotivated progression through experience. It also becomes less and less clear precisely what Augie's real problem is. We know that he has, as he says, a lot of opposition in him and that he refuses to lead a "disappointed life." Like Holden Caulfield he wants a life in which he can accept the full risks of his humanity, but he also wants a specific fate and function, a destiny worthy of his talents and ideals. In David Riesman's terms, he appears, at first glance, to be an "inner-directed" man holding out against the conformist pressures of an "other-directed" society, but it would be truer to say that he is "inner-directed" in temperament but not in aim and that he is holding out against an "inner-directed" society of strongly ambitious and acquisitive aims, the kind of society which we had in this country up until roughly the beginning of World War II. Nevertheless, the point of Augie's life, the point of his resistance, and, therefore, his point as a character, are all strongly ambiguous. He holds out, but in the name of what we never really know.

There is a sense in which it might be argued that Augie both as a character and as a social type is an example of what happens when the individual loses, or is unable to find, a moral purpose, an "inner-directed" goal. All of Augie's adventures are, in a way, pragmatic conquests, attempts to confirm through the application again and again of the test of experience a truth and a vision of reality which ought to come from within and be imposed upon experience. His situation is such that he is able to see validity everywhere, particularly in the lives which those around him have settled for. But the problem he poses as a fictional character is that, as a man committed to nothing, he can have no dramatic centrality; his conflict with society can never be really intense or meaningful because there is nothing at stake, no price of spiritual opposition which might endow him with tragic or pathetic value. This, it seems to me, is the vitiating paradox behind him and his story as a whole. He is empty and without commitment and, in keeping with the rule of decorum and the truth of his social situation and Mr. Bellow's theme, he must be so. But his emptiness is his dramatic ruin, just as it is the ruin of nearly all the characters in recent American fiction. The force of the fall from innocence, of the failure of an heroic design, has given way to the surly spasm of futility and what has been called "the merely middle-class emotion of embarrassment."

It is perhaps because Mr. Bellow subconsciously sensed Augie's inadequacy as a character that he sought through his style to impose upon his material an almost fearsome significance, a disguise of acute profundity, allusion, and paradox, suggesting that behind or above the people of the novel there hangs a thick cloud of metaphysical, philosophical, and historical truth in relation to which their thoughts and actions have meanings more sublime than any that may appear on the surface. One can in fact say that it is the style alone that preserves the novel from the purely naturalistic stereotype, that keeps it from being simply a chronicle of the adventures of an educated Studs Lonigan. It is the style, in particular, which suggests through its images and metaphors that there is a philosophically informed dimension to Augie's development. It creates around him an aura of speculation and examination, so that throughout nearly the whole of his progress, we continue to believe that he is truly engaged in a struggle to choose among fantastically complicated metaphysical alternatives, and that at the end his revelation and ours will come. But as the concrete basis for Augie's development moves farther and farther away from the gaseous invertebrate metaphysic of the style, the style is forced to accomplish more and more, until finally it is required to create all the meaning out of its own resources and to state more meaning than exists in the subject or the scene to be stated.

In the opening sections of the novel the burden imposed upon the style does not strike us as excessive because the world which the style describes is crowded with action and people. There are nevertheless clear symptoms of the excess to come. Here, from the first chapter, is a description of Mr. Kreindl:

> He was an old-time Austro-Hungarian conscript, and there was something soldierly about him: a neck that had strained with pushing artillery wheels, a campaigner's red in the face, a powerful bite in his jaw and gold-crowned teeth, green cockeyes and soft short hair, altogether Napoleonic. His feet slanted out on the ideal of Frederick the Great, but he was about a foot under the required height for guardsmen.

And here is one of Grandma Lausch:

> She took her cigarette case out from under her shawl, she cut a Murad in half with her sewing scissors and picked up the holder. This was still at a time when women did not smoke. Save the intelligentsia—the term she applied to herself. With the holder in her dark little gums between which all her guile, malice, and command issued, she had her best inspirations of strategy. She was as wrinkled as an old paper bag, an autocrat, hard-shelled and jesuitical, a pouncy old hawk of a Bolshevik, her small ribboned gray feet immobile on the shoekit and stool Simon had made in the manual-training class, dingy old wool Winnie, whose bad smell filled the flat, on the cushion beside her.

All this is feverish and overdescribed. The style is aware of so much, so much more than it needs to be aware of, that we feel we are in the presence of monsters. Mr. Kreindl, in particular, is observed so minutely and horrendously that we are carried beyond him into a veritable thicket of gold teeth, strained necks, and green cockeyes. But at this point in the novel the observer is so close to the material, and the material is so thick that we tend to disregard these excesses. Later on, however, when the material thins out, the strain becomes noticeable and offensive. This is especially true of those passages in which the style, lacking the support of specific environmental detail, is required to bear by itself the weight of philosophical speculation. Here is an example from Chapter XXII:

> I have a feeling [Augie says] about the axial lines of life, with respect to which you must be straight or else your existence is merely clownery, hiding tragedy. I must have had a feeling since I was a kid about these axial lines which made me want to have my existence on them, and so I have said "no" like a stubborn fellow to all my persuaders, just on the obstinacy of my memory of these lines, never entirely clear. But lately I have felt these thrilling lines again. When striving stops, there they are as a gift. I was lying on the couch here before and they suddenly went quivering right straight through me. Truth, love, peace, bounty, usefulness, harmony! And all noise and grates, distortion, chatter, distraction, effort, superfluity, passed off like something unreal. And I believe that any man at any time can come back to these axial lines, even if an unfortunate bastard, if he will be quiet and wait it out. The ambition of something special and outstanding I have always had is only a boast that distorts this knowledge from its origin, which is the oldest language, older than the Euphrates, older than the Ganges. At any time life can come together again and man be regenerated, and doesn't have to be a god or public servant like Osiris who gets torn apart annually for the sake of the common prosperity, but the man himself, finite and taped as he is, can still come where the axial lines are. He will be brought into focus. He will live with true joy. Even his pains will be joy if they are true, even his helplessness will not take away his power, even wandering will not take him away from himself, even the big social jokes and hoaxes need not make him ridiculous, even disappointment after disappointment need not take away his love. Death will not be terrible to him if life is not. The embrace of other true people will take away his dread of fast change and short life.

This passage does not raise a question of agreement or disagreement, but it does raise a question of the divisibility of theme and content. We can safely assume that we have here a statement of an important element of the theme which Mr.

Bellow supposed his novel to be developing. There is little evidence in the novel itself, however, that his supposition is correct. This is, in fact, the secret which the abstractness of the style reveals. It is abstract because there exists no specific emotional or social experience to give it body and concreteness. The style is forced to compensate for the insufficiency of the experience on which it is intended to comment by bringing into play such concepts as "truth, love, peace, bounty, usefulness, and harmony," and these, in their irrelevance to the comment of the action itself, testify to the excess of theme over content and the inability of content to meet the responsibility imposed on it by the theme. If Mr. Bellow could have been satisfied simply with the adventures of his hero, with the form which the picaresque tradition made available to him, he would have avoided this problem altogether. But as a serious writer with a strong sense of his responsibility to the issues of our time, he insisted upon trying to do more, and what more he tried to do is expressed in the imperfect union of his theme and his material, his philosophical intention and the incapacity of his material to body it forth; and that is as much a fault of his experience of his time as it is of his talent.

To come at this experience directly and to deal with it with complete success in the novel is perhaps beyond the power of any novelist now living. A more indirect approach appears to be necessary, an approach in which the amount of experience seen is limited by a parochial view, a knowledge of the world in small, which, if faithfully rendered and thoroughly penetrated, may be made to represent the modern world in large. It is the necessity for such a knowledge that probably explains why so many of our younger novelists are writing today out of the Southern experience and tradition. The South for the past several years has been in the phase of social and economic development in which it stands in a sense as an analogical miniature of the situation of America as a whole. It displays in extravagant form all the tensions, conflicts, and evolutionary processes which brought us to our present condition; and its peculiar virtue for the novelist is that, while these processes have, for the most part, worked themselves out elsewhere in the country, they continue to operate in the South and continue, therefore, to throw into sharply dramatic juxtaposition those elements of natural setting, traditional conduct, class disorientation, and personal morality which help to constitute the generalizing power of a literature. The agrarian background and traditional social arrangement of the South have given it an abundance of distinct class types, each with separate manners and histories, and to these have been added new types produced out of the belated Southern industrial revolution. Taken together, these tend to make for discord, bizarre and ludicrous relationships, incongruities of class displacement and propinquity, all of which are again productive of dramatic material.

In an early issue of *The Paris Review* Mr. William Styron was asked to comment on this general question of the South in relation to the state of literature at the present time. His interviewers inquired if he thought it was true that in most of the so-called Southern novels the reactions of the characters are universal. Mr. Styron replied that

> . . . that universal quality comes far more from a single writer's mind and his individual spirit than from his background. Faulkner is a writer of extraordinary stature more because of the great breadth

of his vision than because he happened to be born in Mississippi. All you have to do is read one issue of the *Times Book Review* to see how much junk comes out regularly from south of the Mason-Dixon line, along with the good stuff. I have to admit, though, that the South has a definite literary tradition, which is the reason it probably produces a better quality of writing, proportionately. Perhaps it's just true that Faulkner, if he had been born in, say, Pasadena, might very well still have had that universal quality of mind, *but* instead of writing *Light in August* he would have gone into television or written universal ads for Jantzen bathing suits.

Mr. Styron was asked next why he thought the Southern literary tradition exists at all.

Well, first [he said] there's that old heritage of biblical rhetoric and story-telling. Then the South simply provides such wonderful material. Take, for instance, the conflict between the ordered Protestant tradition, the fundamentalism based on the Old Testament, and the Twentieth Century—movies, cars, television. The poetic juxtaposition you find in this conflict—a crazy colored preacher howling those tremendously moving verses from *Isaiah,* 40, while riding around in a maroon Packard. It's wonderful stuff and comparatively new, too, which is perhaps why the renaissance of Southern writing coincided with the last few decades of the machine age. If Faulkner had written in the 1880's he would have been writing no doubt safely within the tradition, but his novels would have been genteel novels, like those of George Washington Cable or Thomas Nelson Page. In fact, the modern South is such powerful material that the author runs the danger of capturing the local color and feeling that's enough. He gets so bemused by decaying mansions that he forgets to populate them with people. I'm beginning to feel that it's a good idea for writers who come from the South, at least some of them, to break away a little from all them magnolias.

A few years ago *The Hopkins Review,* which was headquartered in Baltimore and had, therefore, a natural bias, conducted a lengthy symposium on the situation of letters in the South, parts of which were later published in book form under the title *Southern Renaissance*. In the course of the discussion the question of the source of Faulkner's genius was repeatedly raised and, as might be expected, repeatedly answered in a way that reflected most favorably on the advantages of his Southern birth and upbringing. While I did not entirely subscribe to some of the opinions that were brought forward, I was sufficiently caught up in the spirit of the occasion to try out the subject on a Southern friend of mine. "What is it that Faulkner has?" I asked him. "Great talent, yes, but also close and living contact with just about the only culture left in America where people still have personality, still live by a semblance of order and dogma, and are, therefore, easily translatable into fictional terms. Or for another example, take Penn Warren's *All the King's Men*. Go through it page by page and try to decide where it gets its great quality of life. From image after image, scene after scene, depicting the richness and complexity and color and tension of Southern life pretty much as it actually exists and, of course, as it impinges upon and is dramatized within the sensibility of Jack Burden." My friend countered with a question: "Where do you think all this richness and complexity and color and tension *is?*" My answer today would be: in the novel. That is the only place it can possibly be if it is to exist and we are ever to get at it. But where it began by being was in the quality and content of Penn Warren's creative imagination. *All the King's Men* was simply the symbolic and verbal vesture of what that imagination was able to imagine and project into artistic form. But the creative imagination cannot exist and continue to imagine in a vacuum, although as we look about us it may appear that a great many imaginations are struggling to do so. It must have access of a deeply generic kind to a body of living experience from which it can derive its dramatic energy and the materials for the images it produces. It must always form, with the raw shapes and appearances of the natural world, as well as with the structured and mannered life of men in the social world, a working partnership which does not differ fundamentally from the sort of partnership so vulgarly exploited by the imagination of the writer of cheap journalism.

This is to say that while I am absolutely certain that Charlotte Brontë wrote *Jane Eyre,* I am equally certain that nineteenth-century Calvinist England coauthored it. On the other hand, while I have good evidence for believing that a person named James Jones actually exists, I continue to believe, on the far greater evidence of his novel *From Here to Eternity,* that James Jones is really a pseudonym for the peacetime United States Army. As for Faulkner and Warren, I attribute the coauthorship of their novels to the South, which, aside from certain ailing portions of the moral universe of New England, happens to be the only section of the country left where, as I have said, there is still a living tradition and a usable myth, where there are still vestiges of an entrenched class authority upon which it is possible, to the great benefit of the novelist, for Northerners to encroach, and where, against the background of Spanish moss, scrub pines, broken-down shanties, and deserted mansions, the suffering of the Negro provides the framework of guilt so essential to our peculiar brand of modern tragedy.

One might in fact say that the only really new vitality to

enter the American novel since the war years has been provided by the South, particularly through the work of those writers who have been concerned with it in its relation to the experience of childhood. I suspect that there are a number of good reasons why this is so, not the least of them being the fact that many of the writers I speak of—Carson McCullers, for example, and Mr. Styron, Truman Capote, and William Goyen—grew up in the South and, now that they are in exile from it, have cause to remember that they had their most intense imaginative life there. In the South it seems that the sensitive child is faced early in life with a grim alternative: either he must live inside his imagination a great part of the time, or he must surely go mad. The South hurts him into the habits of mind congenial to fiction, precisely as mad Ireland hurt William Butler Yeats into poetry. This may explain why it appears that nearly every Southerner who preserves his sanity into adulthood emigrates to New York and becomes a novelist.

Of course almost any experience is dramatic to a sensitive child, and in times of crisis and confusion, when the mature world has become too muddled or frightened or hypocritical to be easily presented in fiction, writers have always taken advantage of the dramatic resources of childhood. But just any childhood will not do. Everything depends on where it is spent. One notices, for instance, how much better a novel Mrs. McCullers was able to make out of the childhoods of her little girls in *The Heart Is a Lonely Hunter* and *Member of the Wedding* than Mr. Salinger was able to make out of the gawky Northern adolescence of Holden Caulfield. Holden's irreverent sensibility is posed against a moral world of New York urban life which scarcely exists dramatically because it is neither very moral nor very tangible. But Mrs. McCullers's characters, however unsatisfactory they may be in other respects, are always located in a world. F. Jasmine in *Member of the Wedding* does little more than sit on a lap through a large part of the book, but at least the lap she sits on belongs to a Negro maid, and that anchors her in the center of a way of life. In *The Heart Is a Lonely Hunter,* Mrs. McCullers's finest novel, the girl Mick is not only anchored; she is hemmed in on all sides by characters out of native Southern life who are symbolic extensions of her central difficulty, which is loneliness. Unlike Holden Caulfield she has a whole set of suitable dramatic equivalents for her feelings. The stage for her is crowded with people, and around and behind them she has the great vitality, richness, and oddity of the Southern spirit and environment to react to and escape from. This same spirit and environment, furthermore, form the content of the magnificently sensitive prose in which her story is presented. The scene describing the deaf-mute Singer's train trip, for example, could not have been written without the South, if only because it is largely the South which the scene describes.

Outside the dirty windows there was the brilliant midsummer countryside. The sun slanted in strong, bronze-colored rays over the green fields of the new cotton. There were acres of tobacco, the plants heavy and green like some monstrous jungle weed. The orchards of peaches with the lush fruit weighting down the dwarfed trees. There were miles of pastures and tens of miles of wasted, washed-out land abandoned to the hardier weeds. The train cut through deep green pine forests where the ground was covered with the slick brown needles and the tops of the trees stretched up virgin and tall into the sky. And farther, a long way south of the town, the cypress swamps—with the gnarled roots of the trees writhing down into the brackish waters, where tropical water flowers blossomed in dankness and gloom. Then out again into the open beneath the sun and the indigo-blue sky.

This is no mere description of landscape. In the final sense, it is a moral commentary, and it is possible only in a place where landscape and the evil of the human heart still retain their primitive moral connection.

Mr. Styron, who is to my mind the most accomplished member of the younger group of Southern novelists, has repeatedly argued that his *Lie Down in Darkness* could have been set in any section of the country. He says in the interview from which I have previously quoted: "Only certain things in the book are particularly Southern. I used leit-motifs—the Negroes, for example—that run throughout the book, but I would like to believe that my people would have behaved the way they did anywhere. The girl Peyton, for instance, didn't have to come from Virginia. She would have wound up jumping from a window no matter where she came from." It seems to me that one reading of his novel is enough to convince one that Mr. Styron is quite mistaken. The Southern elements of the novel—particularly the elements of fundamentalist religion, regionalist guilt, and the contrast of races—are, in fact, so powerful that if anything they seem excessive to the motives of the characters and perpetually to overpower them. This is one of the ways in which *Lie Down in Darkness* differs from *The Adventures of Augie March*. In the latter, the action which Augie takes is insufficient to the philosophical motive which Mr. Bellow attributes to him. In the former, the characters are swept along by a complex of forces stronger than motive and beyond or beneath philosophy. The domestic tensions of misunderstanding and jealousy are only the ostensible causes of the disintegration of the Loftis family. Behind them are larger and more insidious disorders. Behind Milton's father-guilt and incest-guilt is the whole Southern blood-guilt. Behind Helen's jealousy and Puritanism is the timeless Southern gentlewoman madness, the madness that comes from too much in-breeding, too much Negro fear, too much sexual neglect. Behind Peyton's father-complex is a century of paternalism and man-hatred and sexual masochism. And all these drive the Loftises to ruin and give them a dramatic size and intensity greater than in themselves they have any right to possess. Around them, furthermore, is the Southern environment, an environment crowded, as it is for Mrs. McCullers, with objects and instances evocative of evil, hence, expressive and correlative of their own evil.

> Halfway between the railroad station and Port Warwick proper . . . the marshland, petering out in disconsolate, solitary clumps of cattails, yields gradually to higher ground. Here, bordering the road, an unsightly growth of weeds takes over, brambles and briars of an uncertain dirty hue which, as if with terrible exertion, have struggled through the clay to flourish now in stunted gray profusion, bending and shaking in the wind. The area adjacent to this stretch of weeds is bleakly municipal in appearance: it can be seen from the road, and in fact the road eventually curves and runs through it. Here there are great mounds of garbage; a sweet vegetable odor rises perpetually on the air and one can see—from the distance faintly iridescent—whole swarms of carnivorous flies blackening the garbage and maybe a couple of proprietary rats, propped erect like squirrels, and blinking sluggishly, with mild, infected eyes, at some horror-stricken Northern tourist. . . . Below was a brackish creek, foul with sewage and hostile to all life save for great patches of algae the color of green pea soup, where dragonflies darted and hovered, suspended from the sunny air as if by invisible threads . . . somewhere there had been a silly story about the creek—about a Negro

convict who had fallen into the stream and been drowned and who, since the body, mysteriously, was never recovered, had reappeared from the creek at night on each anniversary of his death, covered with scum and slobbering horribly at the mouth as he prowled the town in search of beautiful white women to ravish and to drag back to the unspeakable depths of his grave.

This is the natural material with which the South provides Styron. Through it he is able to respond to and project back into language those intricate relationships between fictional setting and human agony which, at least since Hardy's heath and Conrad's sea, have formed the heart of some of our finest novels. Opposed to this world, in the moral terms of the novel, is the world of the urban North, the world of discontinuity, loneliness, psychoanalysis, nervous breakdown, the world you are exiled to and give up your sanity to, the world in which the environment has nothing to do with the self or with feeling or with life. It is significant that it is after she marries and goes North that Peyton becomes overtly psychotic, undergoes treatment, then kills herself. It is also significant that the section of the novel having to do with her Northern experience is presented in the form of interior monologue. The environment now has no relation to the personal world. The only sense of identity one can get is through talking to one's self. This is the environment at the back of both *Catcher in the Rye* and *The Adventures of Augie March;* and it is perhaps only a slight oversimplification to say that had it been richer, more complicated, more personal, and more dramatic, those novels would have possessed a texture of scene and place more nearly in keeping with the texture of their portraits of people and their philosophical implications.

SIX

Hemingway: the etiquette of the berserk

I MUST CONFESS that I was unable to share in the generally wild enthusiasm occasioned by the appearance of Hemingway's most recent book, *The Old Man and the Sea.* It was indeed a remarkable advance over his previous novel, *Across the River and into the Trees;* and it had a purity of line and a benignity, a downright saintliness, of tone which seemed to indicate not merely that he had sloughed off his former emotional fattiness, but that he had expanded and deepened his spiritual perspective in a way that we could not help but find extraordinary. But one must take care not to push these generosities too far, if only because they spill over so easily into that excess of blind charity we all tend to feel for Hemingway each time he pulls out of another slump and attains to the heroism of simply writing well once again. It should be possible for us to honor him for his amazing recuperative powers and his new talent for quasi-religious revelation and still be able to see that it is not for either of these qualities that his new book must finally be valued, but for the degree of its success in meeting the standards set down by his own best previous achievement as an artist. I have these standards in mind when I say that *The Old Man and the Sea* seems to me a work of distinctly minor Hemingway fiction.

I came to this conclusion after noticing, first of all, that the style of the book, in spite of its antiseptic clarity and restraint, is oddly colorless and flat, as if there were nothing sufficiently strong within its subject to resist it at any point and provoke it into fully alert dramatic life. In the best of the early Hemingway one always felt that the prose had been forced out under great pressure through a tight screen of opposing psychic tensions; and one read it with the same taut apprehensiveness, the same premonition of hugely impending catastrophe, as that with which it was written—quite as if one were picking one's way with the author through an uncleared minefield of language. But now the prose—to change the figure once again—has a fabricated quality, as if it had been shipped into the book by some manufacturer of standardized Hemingway parts.

It soon becomes clear, however, that this weakness of style is merely a symptom of a far more serious weakness in the thematic possibilities of the material itself. The theme of the strong man—Harry Morgan, Colonel Cantwell, or Santiago—struggling to survive amid the hostile pressures of a purely physical world has never been the central theme of Hemingway's greatest fiction; in fact, when one thinks back over his recent novels, one is tempted to conclude that it fails him miserably as a central theme each time he tries to use it in anything more ambitious than a short story. What has always served Hemingway best has been the theme of the shell-shocked, traumatic hero struggling through his code of conduct to preserve himself not from physical but from psychic destruction. This was the theme of his great early work; and it provided him with a formula for dramatic success on which he has never been able to improve.

In the relatively few years since American criticism began devoting serious attention to the contemporary novel, we have learned to be content with two standard approaches to the problem of Hemingway and the code of his hero. The first approach treats of the code as an index of Hemingway's moral perversion, his dumb-ox compromise with the demands of a healthily intellectual and ethical life. The second treats of it as an etiquette of burly fastidiousness by means of which his characters survive in a universe made monstrous by the death of all reasonable, beneficent gods.

For the purposes of rational discussion it should be possible to rule the first approach out of order, simply as an early superficial approach that was not very sensible. But when we come to the second, we discover ourselves in the predicament of having to grant it sense at the same time that we find it wanting in real sensibility. The fact of the matter is that the approach to the code as merely etiquette will kill us yet, if we do not realize soon that the code may be taken as etiquette only at first glance, that in the final consideration what is etiquette for the characters is for Hemingway the artistic convention or formula out of which his novels derive their richest and subtlest effects of dramatic irony.

When Wyndham Lewis observed that the typical Hemingway hero is a man "things are done to," he was undoubtedly thinking of the impression we get of that hero as we watch him suffering and enduring through the course of the typical Hemingway novel. But if we are to understand the operation of the code as both etiquette and dramatic formula, we must begin farther back than Lewis began and conceive of the hero not merely as a man "things are done to" but as a man to whom a great many things have already been done. This is a more precise description of him as he appears to us at the opening of the typical Hemingway novel; and it is here, in the peculiar effects upon him of things already done, of suffering already endured, long before the commencement of any suffering he may be required to endure in the novel itself, that we discover our first clue to the mystery of the code.

For Hemingway's two best heroes, Jake Barnes and Frederic Henry, this antecedent suffering was the result of war; and the effect of this suffering was first physical and then psychic trauma. Jake is introduced at the beginning of *The Sun Also Rises* as having been sexually mutilated by a wound. At the beginning of *A Farewell to Arms* Frederic has already spent two strenuous years at the front. Each has been initiated by violence, Jake through direct physical contact with it and Frederic through long vicarious association with it; and each has made his separate peace, his private adjustment to the problem of survival. Onto the background of incessant war they have both learned to project an artificial system of checks and balances, a kind of psychic radar screen composed of propitiatory rituals and sacred signs, which, if rigorously maintained, will preserve them at least temporarily from destruction. There is, of course, no ultimate escape from the violence against which their defenses are raised; for it is both universal and abstract, and it is completely unselective in its choice of victims. "It kills the very good and the very gentle and the very brave impartially. If you are none of these you can be sure it will kill you too but there will be no special hurry." All one can do in the face of such indiscriminate killing is make certain that one is not very good or very gentle or very brave; and, luckily, that is exactly the assurance that the code provides.

Within the magic circle of the code Jake and Frederic are permitted the luxury of retaining intact the values of a successful life. They may believe in love, honor, goodness, truth, gentleness, dignity, and bravery; for these are actually the values on which the code is founded. But the code is required to function amid the harsh facts of reality; and the harshest fact of all is that, however good these values may be in themselves, they can never with safety be openly asserted in a world dominated by a lawless violence. Jake and Frederic may possess these values, but only so long as they possess them implicitly and say nothing about them, or are careful to express them concretely and only in ways that have been ritualized by the code—as, for example, in sexual intercourse, which is ritualized love, or in simple, manly forbearance, which is ritualized goodness and dignity, or in bullfighting, which is ritualized bravery and a way of courting death with honor. To assert these values openly, however, is to uproot them from the concrete, physical circumstances of ritual and to consign them to the realm of the abstract, where they will be infected with the violence of the world and become destructive. For Jake and Frederic the overt assertion of any one of the implicit values of the code represents a giving of the self, a loss of will and consciousness, which is tantamount to death.

Dr. Carl Jung, in his book *Psychology and Religion,* has said that

> . . . consciousness must have been a very precarious thing in its beginnings. In relatively primitive societies we can still observe how easily consciousness is lost. One of the "perils of the soul" is, for instance, the loss of a soul. This is a case of a part of the psyche becoming unconscious again. Another example is the amok condition, the equivalent of the berserk condition in the Germanic saga. This is a more or less complete trance, often accompanied by devastating social effects. Even an ordinary emotion can cause a considerable loss of consciousness. Primitives therefore cherish elaborate forms of politeness, speaking with a hushed voice, laying down their weapons, crouching, bowing the head, showing the palms. Even our own forms of politeness still show a "religious" observation of possible psychical dangers. We propitiate the fates by wishing magically for a good day. It is not good form to keep the left hand in your pocket or behind your back when shaking hands. If you want to be particularly propitiating you use both hands. Before people of great authority we bow with uncovered head, i.e., we offer our head unprotected in order to propitiate the powerful one, who might easily fall suddenly a prey to a fit of uncontrollable violence. In war dances primitives can become so excited that they may shed blood. . . . Primitives recognize the ever-lurking possibility of psychical dangers, and the attempts and procedures employed to diminish the risks are numerous.

"Even an ordinary emotion can cause a considerable loss of consciousness. Primitives therefore cherish elaborate forms of politeness, speaking with a hushed voice, laying down their weapons, crouching, bowing the head, showing the palms"— in short, reproducing in ritual form the quiescent attributes

of the sternly conscious mind. We may add to this what we know of other primitive practices designed to exorcise evil. Sir James Frazer, for example, speaks of the tribal custom of pantomime, in which, in the form of religious ceremony or dance, the event most dreaded by the tribe is represented as actually happening, but happening in a way which makes it acceptably familiar and therefore purgative of the fear that is attached to it in life.

Recognizing as we do the peculiarly instinctual nature of Hemingway's art, it should not come as too great a surprise to us to discover close parallels between his creative processes and those of primitive man. The code of his heroes is clearly the symbolic construction of a psychic barricade erected against one of the primary perils of his soul—the loss of consciousness leading to a lawless, amok, or berserk condition. His art, when it is truest and most organically his, is a pantomimic rendering of a series of events which result in the breakdown of this barricade and in the subsequent loss of consciousness which he so greatly dreads. When the breakdown and loss occur, the emotion of fear is purged and the full dramatic energy of the art is released.

Mr. Philip Young in his recent short study of Hemingway gives a psychoanalytical interpretation of certain of Hemingway's typical artistic effects which comes very close to the view I am attempting to develop here. Mr. Young takes as the generative moment of the Hemingway trauma the famous night of July 8, 1918, at Fossalta di Piave, the night of the big wound when, like his hero Frederic Henry, Hemingway felt himself die and his soul leave his body. "I died then," he later recalled. "I felt my soul or something coming right out of my body, like you'd pull a silk handkerchief out of a pocket by one corner." Mr. Young believes that from this moment dates Hemingway's obsessive preoccupation with death, his need to return compulsively, in violation of Freud's "pleasure principle," over and over again to the scenes of his injuries, and his tendency, furthermore, before submitting to death symbolically through his heroes, to occupy himself with vicarious dying—with witnessing and participating in many wars, many feats of daring, many bullfights. Drawing on the authority of Otto Fenichel's *Psychoanalytical Theory of Neurosis,* Mr. Young goes on to demonstrate how the experience of the big wound produced in Hemingway the traumatic and repetitive mechanism of decorum and self-control which in his novels takes the form of the code. "Trauma," says Fenichel, almost in paraphrase of Jung, "creates fear of every kind of tension . . . because even a little influx of excitement may have the effect of 'flooding' the patient," or, in Jung's terms, causing him to lose consciousness and go berserk. Nevertheless, "the patient cannot free himself from thinking about the (traumatic) occurrence over and over again," as both Hemingway and his heroes do. There comes a time, however, when the trauma itself has done its damage, and when the patient "has to find new and better ways of adaptation. This . . . consists in nothing more than a complicated system of bindings and primitive discharges," or, in Hemingway's case, in a process of gradual mastery of the traumatic "excitation" leading to a certain suppression and impoverishment of the personality and, finally, to a state of what Fenichel calls "primitivation" and Young identifies as Hemingway's familiar primitivism. Mr. Young's approach is illuminating as far as it goes, but it does no more than provide the terms for the analysis which I am attempting here to undertake. What it fails to do is bring Hemingway's traumatic experience fully to bear on the dramatic pattern of his novels and to demonstrate the central fact that Hemingway in each of his best novels returns compulsively to the circumstances which induced his trauma, reproduces in the form of artistic pantomime the loss of soul or consciousness, the psychic death, which he himself experienced in those circumstances, shows how this loss occurs in the symbolic terms of the breakdown of the code, and achieves, through the process, a purgation of his own sense of fear as well as the dramatic climax of his art.

We might well suspect this somewhat extraliterary view of the code if we did not have before us the evidence of the two novels of Hemingway's—*The Sun Also Rises* and *A Farewell to Arms*—which stand above all his others in quality because, in them, the code and the circumstances and consequences of its destruction are presented and objectified in the purest possible form. It is in them, furthermore, that, in strict keeping with the nature of the code, the destructive agent is most clearly seen to arise out of the overt and violent assertion of some value on which the code is actually based but which it is against the law of the code to affirm.

In *The Sun Also Rises* Robert Cohn, the man who behaves badly by daring to admit his feelings, is the bearer of the destructive agent; and it is part of the consuming irony of the novel that the feelings he dares to admit are exactly those which Jake and Brett would like to express if *they* dared and if Jake's wound did not make it impossible for them to do so. The wound may be taken as a symbolic representation of the taboo which the code has imposed upon such feelings. In a passage of dialogue between Brett and Count Mippipopolous early in the novel this taboo is somewhat obliquely suggested by Brett.

> "Doesn't anything ever happen to your values?" Brett asked.
> "No. Not any more."
> "Never fall in love?"
> "Always," said the count. "I am always in love."
> "What does that do to your values?"

The count replies that love, too, has a place in his values; but since love is forbidden in Jake's and Brett's values, the wound is there to prevent them from having it and to force their emotion into channels of expression which their values do approve—Brett into sexual promiscuity and Jake into manly forbearance.

In the beginning the Pamplona fiesta is another approved channel: the drinking is carefully ritualized; the talk is good; and the weather is fair, as it always is for Hemingway when life is being lived according to the rules. But as the excitement of the holiday grows more intense, as the drinking spills over into drunkenness and street dancing, and as Jake, Brett, Mike, Bill, and Robert Cohn are caught up in a mounting tide of uncontrollable emotion, the fiesta becomes a setting of nightmare violence, a frenzied correlative action, for the berserk behavior by which Cohn brings about the destruction of the code.

It is interesting to see that as this occurs, all the elements attending on such destruction are actualized in the form of concrete, dramatic events. On the morning the first signs of disaster appear, the weather changes, and it starts to rain.

Mike, to the great disgust of the *aficionado* Montoya, breaks the rules by behaving badly toward the bullfighter Romero. Cohn, after having been humiliated once too often by the unfeeling Brett, knocks down Jake and Mike and has a vicious fight with Romero. Immediately afterwards, a Spaniard is gored to death by a bull, not, significantly, in the ring where his death would be in accordance with the rules, but in the runway leading to the ring. Coming back to his hotel after the fight with Cohn, Jake feels unreal, as if he were walking in a dream; and this, like the whole nightmare of the fiesta itself, symbolizes the dreaded loss of consciousness which accompanies the death of the code or the psychic death of the self.

> Walking across the square to the hotel everything looked new and changed. I had never seen the trees before. I had never seen the flagpoles before, nor the front of the theatre. It was all different. I felt as I felt once coming home from an out-of-town football game. I was carrying a suitcase with my football things in it, and I walked up the street from the station in the town I had lived in all my life and it was all new. They were raking the lawns and burning the leaves in the road, and I stopped for a long time and watched. It was all strange. Then I went on, and my feet seemed to be a long way off, and everything seemed to come from a long way off, and I could hear my feet walking a great distance away. I had been kicked in the head early in the game. It was like that crossing the square.

This is also a moment of insight and conversion, when illusion is penetrated and reality revealed. But it is more importantly a surrogate form of the moment of death, and it is scarcely an accident that the words Jake uses here echo those of Frederic Henry's description of his wounding, as well as Hemingway's description of his own wounding. At any rate, following on this scene, as Cohn, who has been the agent of the death of the code, leaves Pamplona in defeat, the gored Spaniard's funeral procession moves through the streets on its way to the railroad station. In this fashion the pantomime is completed, the fear is purged, and all the elements of the code ritual are thoroughly objectified in the art.

At the beginning of *A Farewell to Arms* Frederic Henry's relations with the war are strikingly like Jake's relations with Brett. As long as the war is fought according to the rules, it is essential to Frederic's psychic survival to be attached to it and to respect its values; but it is equally essential that he maintain his spectatorial role with regard to it and that he respect its values in his own way. He will do his job conscientiously; but he will not be brave or honorable or glorious or self-sacrificing. These are dangerous abstractions of the true values of war, and are "obscene beside the concrete names of villages, the numbers of roads, the names of rivers, the numbers of regiments and the dates." They are like love as opposed to sex, goodness as opposed to forbearance, nightmare as opposed to good clean daylight. They force the mind away from essential experience and make one uncomfortably aware of the violent world outside that sometimes haunts one in sleep. It is only by living within the code that one can remain intact and completely, safely awake.

But in the Isonzo bombardment the war itself becomes violent, breaks the rules, and wounds Frederic; and, characteristically enough, it is at the moment of wounding that he has the sense of losing consciousness or self which, like Jake's sense of unreality, is the objective equivalent of the breakdown of the code. "I tried to breathe but my breath would not come and I felt myself rush bodily out of myself and out and out and out . . . and I knew I was dead. Then I floated, and instead of going on I felt myself slide back. I breathed and I was back." Later on, in the bewildering chaotic convoy movement back through the mud and rain from Caporetto, the destruction of the code by insane violence is again objectified; and, significantly, it is the *carabinieri,* those staunch defenders of the abstract values of a military action now gone berserk, who force Frederic to take the plunge into the river which purges him of his connections with the war altogether.

After his wounding on the Isonzo and the simultaneous breakdown of the code, Frederic begins to affirm overtly his hitherto forbidden love for Catherine Barkley; and with the last of his obligations swept away in the river, the future is now clear for its complete fulfillment. But unfortunately, with the code no longer in force, there is also nothing to prevent the rampant violence of the world from destroying that love; in fact, in Hemingway's terms, this is fated to happen to all emotions that are pursued purely and for their own sake outside the limits of the code. So, in the closing pages of the novel, we are confronted with the irony for which the earlier dramatic manipulation of the code has prepared us: with the flight to Switzerland the lovers have won their freedom; but they have left behind the ritualized faith which alone can make freedom tenable, and so they are condemned. Catherine must die; and Frederic, who has already experienced one death and been reborn and rebaptized, must die again.

In the three novels just preceding *The Old Man and the Sea* the code, in the sense that I have described it up to now, almost entirely disappears; and with it disappears the whole pantomimic ritual in terms of which the destruction of the code was formerly symbolized in loss of consciousness or psychic death, and as a result of which the psychic death was formerly dramatized in concrete instances of violence and physical death. Through some premature sagging of Hemingway's creative muscles, what used to be a system of fine internal tensions working their way dramatically to the surface becomes, in these novels, a fatty tissue of dead matter lying inertly in the open.

Harry Morgan in *To Have and Have Not* is a comic facsimile of the earlier Hemingway heroes. He is tough, taciturn, hard-drinking, and sexually athletic; but where these attributes were, in his predecessors, the ritualized forms of inner virtues that threatened at every moment to become violently and destructively overt, they are in him simply part of the static military equipment with which he does physical battle with a physical world in the face of certain physical death. The destructive agent is centered not in him or in his personal surroundings but in the rich, in whom, for the dramatic purposes of the novel and the psychic purposes of the code, it has no right to be centered. Consequently, when Morgan is finally destroyed, he is destroyed on the outside only. There is no psychic death because there has been no psychic life; and what little emotion is purged is not Morgan's or Hemingway's fear of an abstract horror, but simply our own fear that a doom so mechanically instigated will be, as it is, equally mechanically sealed.

In *For Whom the Bell Tolls* the destructive agent is also centered in an outside force, although this fact is rather well concealed by Hemingway's skillful use of rhetoric, polemics, and interior monologue, as well as by the presence of displaced and largely inactive elements of the old code formula. There is, for example, the familiar theme of loyalty to the common cause of the group, a loyalty which manifests itself in the same old reticences and courtesies. There is also the trapped-love motif, the tenderness of which is deepened by the violence which crowds close around it; and there is even the device of the code violator—in this case, Pablo—who, like Robert Cohn, is meant to destroy the code and let the violence in. But the difficulty is that the code of the group—or, more correctly, the pseudo code—is set against *physical* and not abstract violence. It is physical death at the hands of the fascists which Jordan and the others face; and the only result of Pablo's treachery is to bring that death a little closer. There is, consequently, no more room for the full dramatic formula of the code to work than there was in *To Have and Have Not*—no moment in the action when the violation of the code can be objectified in the terms of a correlative physical nightmare.

In view of all that has been said about *Across the River and into the Trees,* it would seem pointless to say more, particularly when one is able to offer nothing beyond an endorsement of the prevailing, although perhaps not the fashionable, critical verdict. But it may be useful if I lend the emphasis of my present argument to one fact about the book—that in it the slackening process which began for Hemingway with *To Have and Have Not* reaches a sad and ludicrous conclusion; and all that was once hard, intense, and rigidly controlled disintegrates into blatant self-burlesque. The code—if one can call it that—is now literally and consciously the joke-etiquette and tipsy mumbo-jumbo of an imaginary barroom secret society. The trapped-love motif, with its great dramatic potential, has crumbled into the incestuous pawings of a lonely old man who has nothing better to do while he waits to die. The emotion which it used to be death to utter and which, therefore, played over the agonies of physical suffering and frustrated love with great irony, has been diluted and sentimentalized into the querulous self-pity of the infirm. All the fatuities of which Hemingway has in the past shown himself to be occasionally capable—in *The Green Hills of Africa* and *Death in the Afternoon* as well as in *To Have and Have Not*—are fully consummated before the embarrassed eye.

Finally, in *The Old Man and the Sea,* the purely physical takes over altogether; and we have nothing but the naked contest of strength and courage between the aged Santiago and the fish—a drama which, for all its delicacy and depth of execution, is as far below the standard of complexity set by the early novels as *The Sun Also Rises* would be if it consisted of nothing but the bullfights at Pamplona. As for the code, it has diminished to the merest remnant of what it was, is now simply a bit of worrying irritation in the old man's mind over the *hubris* which has driven him to go out too far.

One remembers a bit sadly in reading over this novel Edmund Wilson's comment of nearly fifteen years ago that Hemingway's creative fluctuations are like the workings of the Bourdon gauge which operates on the principle that "a tube which has been curved into a coil will tend to straighten out in proportion as the liquid inside it is subjected to an increasing pressure." At the time Wilson presumably meant the analogy as a compliment to Hemingway's recuperative powers; but today it lends itself to a different interpretation. The tube now, we might say, has long since withstood the maximum pressure it was made to bear and has at last straightened out completely and for good. The tense young man in dramatic flight from the black horror of trauma has faded into the exhausted old man relaxed in an attitude of crucifixion and dreaming of the clear daylight and lions playing on the African coast.

SEVEN

The question of Malcolm Cowley

THE HISTORICAL METHOD in criticism, which over the past several years Malcolm Cowley, among others in this country, has vigorously simplified into popularity, is not one we set much serious stock by, although its lineage is long and, for the most part, distinguished, and its influence in shaping mass standards of literary opinion has always been very great. Its primary appeal for the public mind undoubtedly stems from the fact that throughout its course it has interested itself steadily in something other than literature—in society rather than in art, in the psychology of the producer rather than in the work produced—with the result that it has come to represent a kind of epicurean YMCA for those who have aspired and failed to win membership in the international fraternity of taste.

In the introduction to his *History of English Literature*, published in 1863, Hippolyte Taine, one of the great early

French masters of the historical method, summarized its objectives in the phrase *the moment, the race, and the milieu.* This is to say that the literary work is to be understood as the product of the historical climate of the time, the cultural inheritance of the people, and the current circumstances of the society. In theory, what this represented for Taine, as well as for the members of his immediate circle—Michelet, Renan, Sainte-Beuve—was a system for reducing literature to its chemical components by bringing to bear upon it the methods of the new mechanistic sciences, which were then engaged in reducing the universe to absurdity. But in practice it represented a quasi-critical excuse for trading the rigor of criticism for the security of a ready-made metaphysical cliché into which almost any writer could be crammed and made to fit. Taine's Racine, for example, appears to us not as the dramatist of power whose plays we honor today, but as an effete seventeenth-century courtier who has been bled lily-white to conform with Taine's preconceptions of the seventeenth century. In a similar way, Taine chides Balzac for creating characters who act objectionably and, on occasion, obscenely, but whose sin is not their lack of verisimilitude but simply their failure to act in accordance with a standard of conduct acceptable to the genteel morals of Taine. The supreme question, the question which the best esthetic criticism would always ask: whether the *Comédie humaine* is a valid literary judgment of the contemporary situation, a satisfactorily realized work of art, Taine never gets around to asking, nor does his tradition as a whole know how to formulate it. It is a tradition which has been determined above all to systematize and, if need be, to revise reality to conform with its preconceived image of it; and as is the case with all totalitarian ideologies, what it has been unable to make conform it has exiled or spiritually castrated or simply suppressed.

This tendency in the historical method made it an easy victim of the compulsive philosophical shoplifting which passed for politics in this country during the twenties and thirties. What was desperately called for in those years was a politics capable of viewing all human endeavor, whether in public affairs or the arts, as the product of the interacting forces of history and economics, but one which at the same time held open the possibility that these forces could be brought under control and made subservient to the collectivist and humanitarian aims of the people. This had been the great sustaining vision behind the labor movement from the beginning, and it had reasserted itself in the traumatic idealism that grew up in the first years of the American Depression. Marxism had seemed at the time to provide such a politics in the field of government, and the historical method became its counterpart and, in a sense, its official technique in the field of ideas. The way had earlier been prepared not only by the teachings of Hegel, Marx, and Engels, but in this country by the work of writers like Charles and Mary Beard, Vernon L. Parrington, and to a certain extent, H. L. Mencken and Van Wyck Brooks, each of whom had imposed upon the past his private social, psychological, or moral "reading," cast always in the framework of the programmatic *reductio ad absurdum* of historicism. But by the middle of the thirties, as the full force of the Marxist influence made itself felt, even these staunchly doctrinal approaches began to seem mild and naïve by comparison with the militant mulishness which shortly overcame the thinking of the Left and which brought the exploitation of literature by politics to an apex of madness it has never since been able to attain. Certain of the younger Marxist critics, lacking the learning of their elders and grown impatient with a point of view which stressed only the reciprocal relationship of history and literature, now began to trumpet for a literature not merely reflective of the social scene but charged with reformist comment upon it. The labor of ideological instruction which Taine had performed on the works of Racine and Balzac critics like Michael Gold and Granville Hicks now tried to perform on the works and works-in-progress of Hemingway, Faulkner, Thornton Wilder, and some of the other distinguished writers of the time. While these writers for the most part remained cold to both the threats and the endearments of the Left, others of less conviction were more seriously affected, and there grew up a whole genre of ready-to-wear novels and plays featuring the prescribed stereotype capitalists, who were always bad, and the crowds of decent, clean-cut, idealistic workers who were always depicted at the end marching triumphantly, their picks and shovels on their shoulders, the Internationale on their singing lips, up out of the valley of oppression into the ruddy dawn of the new proletarian tomorrow. One can only speculate on how far this foolishness might have been carried had there not set in, at about the beginning of World War II, a disillusionment with the ideal on which this and other revisionary tendencies in the American Marxist movement had been based, the ideal of the ultimate perfectibility of history or, as Edmund Wilson put it, the belief in man's ability to "impose on the events of the present a pattern of actual direction which will determine the history of the future."

There also came to power during and immediately following World War II a different school of criticism formed out of rebellion against the historical method and taking to itself the biases of the later existentialist philosophies which were then forcing historicism into the discard. This was the esthetic school originated by Coleridge and by Taine's contemporaries Baudelaire and Gourmont and carried forward into the modern era by T. E. Hulme and T. S. Eliot. Younger critics like Allen Tate, R. P. Blackmur, and Kenneth Burke, who had come of age in the political atmosphere of the twenties and thirties and whose talents had early been warmed by the fires of controversy, bypassed the trap of *moment, race, and milieu* and following Eliot began to programmatize a conception of literature as existing in and for itself, to be properly approached through its own symbolic properties, its form and language. Meanwhile, the historical method steadily declined in authority and influence, becoming more and more the critical palliative of the mass reading public and the grubstake of those literary backwoodsmen who spent their time between trips across the wide Missouri haranguing novelists for failing to present a "true" picture of American life and the American business man, and who persisted in trying to hold the cracked mirror of naturalism up to a world which had ceased long before to exist in its terms. Of the best old historical critics only a very few managed to escape this kind of debasement and to continue working productively in the tradition which, in a sense, they had already outlived. Edmund Wilson was one of these, and Malcolm Cowley was another. Wilson, however, was from the beginning something of a special case, for while he remained essentially faithful to the principle of the historical method, his wide range of intellectual interests carried him well beyond its programmatic confines. Cowley, while he has been enriched by the tradition of Baudelaire, has remained intellectually and temperamentally the more resolute historian. In his two book-length works of prose, *Exile's Return* and the present *The Literary Situation,* it is possible to see that his weaknesses are, in very large part, those of the historical method itself, and that his strengths are those which he has brought to his prose out of the resources of his poetic imagination.

Exile's Return, first published in 1934 and reissued in revised and expanded form in 1951, was an autobiographical narrative of development cast in the framework of an historical account of the literary twenties and thirties. But it was first and foremost a work of personal history conceived imaginatively and poetically, with all the vividness of a deeply felt emotional experience. Although it had to do with trends and fashions of thought and conduct, with the moment and milieu of a literary movement, it was dramatized both by the vigor and complexity of the subject itself and by the intensity of Cowley's own participation in it. The trends and fashions were treated as if they were characters in a first-rate fiction—as, for that matter, were the real-life literary figures whose activities afforded the book its wealth of anecdotal material. And since Cowley's concern was not with ideas as such nor with the artistic properties of individual literary works, nothing in his subject defied his poet's talent for reducing experience to the simple, the pictorial, and the concrete. No intellectual abstraction, no call upon his powers of precise critical judgment, forced him to expose the weakness which, on the occasion of his first book of poems *Blue Juniata* published a few years earlier, Allen Tate had found evident in him. "No American at present," said Tate in a *New Republic* review, "writes a more lucid prose than Cowley, and yet it is now clear that prose, certainly critical prose, is not his true medium. His mind is basically concrete and unspeculative; he brings to facts and observations an even, emotional tone that is the mark of a genuine style; but in criticism Cowley's instinct for exact definition is not strong; and the necessity for a certain amount of abstraction only violates the even tone of his style." It was the poet in Cowley who was responsible for the lucid prose of which Tate speaks, and it was because Cowley was able through that prose to personalize and lyricize his historical subject in *Exile's Return* that the book remained free of the defects inherent in his essentially historical method.

But Cowley's handling of a similarly historical subject in *The Literary Situation* gives rise to questions which cannot be so easily or so pleasantly resolved. His subject now is the condition of literature and of the creative spirit in this country at the present time, and, as his thesis demonstrates, that condition is largely one of stasis and retrenchment and is thus not in itself very stimulating. Cowley, furthermore, obviously does not have a sense of being personally caught up in it or emotionally engaged with its issues. His experience of active emotional participation in the literary life apparently came to an end with the period which he documented in *Exile's Return*, and of late years he has retreated more and more into seclusion;

his point of view has grown increasingly elder statesmanish; and his tone has undergone a gradual change from the lyric to the avuncular. What happens now in literature clearly seems to him to be happening to other people and no longer to himself or his friends. His dilemma in this new book, therefore, is that he cannot, on the one hand, count on his subject to dramatize itself through its own dramatic properties, and because he feels no personal or imaginative connection with it, he cannot, on the other hand, count on his poetic gifts to dramatize it for him. He is also up against the difficulty that as his sense of involvement has faded, these gifts, which in the poet are always directly dependent upon such a sense, seem themselves to have faded, leaving him out in the cold with nothing left but a style. It is still the lucid style which Allen Tate admired, but it is no longer lucid in the same way. Where in the past it had the lucidity which the poet achieves in forcing his strong and complex feelings under tension into form, it now appears to have the lucidity of a simple and rather tired view of experience, of complexities shunned and tensions abdicated. In the face of this, Cowley has had in this book to fall back for support upon the only method of prose narration he knows, and that is the horizontal and classificatory method of historicism. Throughout the book he has substituted tabulation for analysis, an enumeration of trends for a definition of causes, categorical labels for critical insights, lists of book titles, statistics on the paper-backed publishing industry, a "natural history" of the personal habits of writers, for a comprehensive synthesis of the facts behind the literary situation today. Perhaps more completely than any other journalistic critic of his generation, Cowley had in his grasp the materials out of which such a synthesis could have been made, for whatever his shortcomings, he has at least *read* the literature of our time and has been required professionally to hold informed opinions on it. Instead, what we get from him is a kind of plodding intellectual peasantry, a rural stubbornness in the face of abstract ideas, a penchant for dropping into his private memory hole whatever he cannot assimilate to his method or fully understand, a compulsion to reduce everything to the hard oversimplicity of bedrock, a compulsion which blinds him to the possibility that bedrock is at best merely a foundation and at worst merely an affectation. His mask is that of the kindly old sharecropper of letters who happens to write when the weather is too inclement for plowing or duck hunting, and while this undoubtedly serves to endear him to the lower orders of his readership, it disserves him badly on those occasions when it is clearly a disguise to cover a certain laziness of mind and a certain queasiness before the moral combat of cognition.

Near the beginning of his book and at intervals throughout it Cowley makes use of another kind of mask which affords us our angle of vision into much of his material and which illustrates far more tellingly than his rusticity of tone the evasive attitude he takes toward his responsibilities as critic. This is the mask of the uninitiated foreign observer—Cowley's choice is a "cultivated Hindu sociologist"—who is stationed at the edge of the current literary arena and through whose innocent eyes Cowley invites us to view with him the spectacle unfolding in its center. By resorting to this mask Cowley provides himself with an excuse for shirking the job of careful and thorough discussion which, if he were doing the seeing through his own eyes, he would be expected to perform. Faced with the problem of exploring in detail the works and trends fundamental to the literary situation, the problem of really taking up the burden of criticism, he is now able through his Hindu proxy to escape into his preferred and more relaxed role of historian and statistician of the simple and the obvious. His typical method is to draw up lists of novels and then to create an illusion of definition by stating that twenty-eight of them have to do with the war in the Pacific, nineteen with homosexuality, and seventy-two with life in the urban slums. "I counted," he informs us at one point, "the romantic or tragic love stories in ten of these earlier books (war novels). Of the affairs that go beyond the category of merely Having Sex, there are four with Italians, two with Germans . . . , two with Frenchwomen (of whom one is half Javanese), one with a Tonkinese, one with a New Zealander, and one with a Japanese. . . ." It would be different if this kind of thing were supplementary to an examination of the real meaning and worth of these novels, but when it constitutes very nearly the whole of what Cowley has to say about them, I believe one has a right to complain. This same approach, or variations of it, vitiates almost to the point of absurdity all those sections of the book having to do with the literary situation as such. It is only in the chapters setting forth the "Natural History of the American Writer," where Cowley is not required to concern himself with more than simple statistics and categories—so many writers live in Connecticut; some writers drink six pints of gin a day, but only when they are engaged on very long work; most of the writers who are not teachers are employed at other jobs; a number of writers are homosexual; at least one is a sadist; a lot are normal—it is only in these chapters that he is as informative and entertaining as one would expect him to be throughout.

After thinking back over Cowley's critical career and setting aside those fine and definitive essays on writers like Hemingway and Faulkner which he has occasionally been able to do, one is forced to conclude that he has suffered increasingly from the effects of trying to simplify his ideas for the benefit of what he obviously considers to be a simple-minded reading public. It is now clear that after more than twenty years of unremitting industry spent in this endeavor, he has at last succeeded in attaining his objective. But we should also remember that Cowley really belongs to a literary period different and older than ours, the period he described so well in *Exile's Return,* when, as Lionel Trilling once remarked, "criticism existed in heroic practical simplicity." I suspect, however, that Cowley should be reminded now, at this crucial stage in his career, that criticism is no longer simple, and that its heroism consists today in facing squarely and intelligently the full complexities of the literary situation in which we live.

EIGHT

Ira Wolfert: the failure of a form

FOR SOME YEARS NOW Ira Wolfert has been building a reputation for literary competence of that rare high kind which is so close to excellence that we must assess it rather as the product of an aspiration strained beyond its means than as a symptom of a talent which has found it more profitable to cheat than to aspire. Although he has had perhaps more opportunity than most men, Mr. Wolfert has never cheated: the impulse behind his aspiration has remained holy. But it is none the less true that his aspiration has been of such quality and directed toward such ends that it has been doomed from the start to exceed his creative grasp. He is the sort of man who probably should never have come to the novel in the first place. He is by nature ill-equipped for it, and perhaps because he senses his inadequacy he is always trying to make it do work it was never meant to do, at least in such hands as his, or to twist it into some hitherto undiscovered form more congenial to his limitations.

What his limitations are must by now be notorious, for he has displayed them to good effect in two novels before his most recent one, *Married Men.* They consist, in brief, of an averageness of mind, a mediocrity of taste, and an obviousness of feeling, all of which have caused him embarrassment in his dealings with the larger philosophical abstractions and the finer complexities of human emotion and behavior. In at least one of his earlier works, however, Mr. Wolfert was able to get around his limitations by the simple strategy of doing nothing to call them forth. When he wrote *Tucker's People,* his first novel, in the early forties, he depended almost entirely on his very superior journalistic gifts—his clear perception of environmental detail, his deep sympathy for and understanding of the various dwarfed personality types which inhabit the modern underworld, and his ability to exploit to great dramatic effect the shade of difference between a fictional account and its constantly intruding factual basis.

Of all his gifts this last probably served him and the novel to best advantage, for it made it virtually impossible for the average reader to see the fiction except through the haze of his emotional response to the social condition against which the fiction was a protest. And the same was true of his reaction to Mr. Wolfert's war novel, *An Act of Love:* he saw it as a glorious confirmation of his most cherished conventional attitudes toward the patriotic fact of war as he was able to observe that fact under the fevered and overblown circumstances of 1945. He did not recognize Mr. Wolfert's fatuousness in that novel, or his oppressively manic view of the joys of dying in battle—if he had, he would have been obliged to recognize them as his own, and that, in 1945, would have amounted to an act of subversion.

Mr. Wolfert's gift for exploiting the moment had seduced the reader into taking a meretricious view of fiction, precisely as it had enabled Mr. Wolfert to elevate meretriciousness to the level of a kind of low literature. I do not say that he did this deliberately; he simply happened to share the attitudes of the great mass of his public. But it did have the effect of forestalling for a long time the critical judgment of his powers as a novelist which we are now compelled to make. For now, in *Married Men,* he has chosen to present, in journalistic form and language but in the terms of a conception far beyond the range of his journalistic gifts, a body of material from which no meretricious influence of timeliness or popular interest can arise to help him.

Mr. Wolfert's material in *Married Men* is no less than the moral and industrial history of a certain imaginary sector of American life in the modern era; or, to put it another way, the novel represents an attempt to analyze on a major scale the politics of the relationship which once existed in this country between the structures of economic class and the structures of the self. That Mr. Wolfert has largely failed in the attempt, or that, in some respects, his is one of the most important failures we have suffered in the novel in recent years, is not for the moment our concern. What should interest us first is his method, for that is the form in which his failure is transmitted to us and the form which, in large measure, his failure takes.

The striking feature of that form is its enormous size: Mr.

Wolfert's failure consists partly in his compulsive inability to make it smaller. The novel runs to slightly more than a thousand pages; and we are told on the jacket that it was revised three times. There can, consequently, be no mistake about it: Mr. Wolfert thought he knew what he was doing and could do no less. But what he thought he knew must escape our immediate comprehension, for in this country, at least in recent times, such garrulity as his has come to be thought of more as an ailment than as a method—the affliction of writers who, having failed to capture their subjects in youth, must resort in middle life to chasing them down through pages of print.

In the European novel, where garrulity is very nearly the grand tradition, we are inclined to accept it or, more often, to ignore it because it is usually inseparable from some great sustaining subject, some vast generalizing conception of man in nature. Even when Dickens and Dostoevski were writing novels to order, which they were not at all above doing, they were careful to write them by the pound rather than by the yard. Their subjects, furthermore, were not something they pursued; they were something they had, as elderly Boston gentlewomen have their hats. But American writers tend to have material rather than subjects, impressions rather than conceptions, feelings rather than emotions; and what they are apt to feel most intensely about is merely themselves. In this respect Mr. Wolfert is no Thomas Wolfe. He is not in the least interested in himself. If anything he is closer, in some of his technical resources, to the Russians. He has a sense of dramatic scene and detail that is nearly Tolstoyan; he even shares somewhat in Tolstoy's great preoccupation with the mechanics of power and its effect on men. But he is what Tolstoy would have been if he had been drugged and imprisoned, chained to a desk and condemned to write endlessly long after he had ceased to think. And his novel is a kind of *War and Peace manqué,* what Tolstoy might have written if he had had merely all that material, all that sweep, and no suitable form in which to make of his material a truly meaningful dramatic subject.

The material of *Married Men* is of two kinds. There is on the one hand the massive narrative itself, documenting in endless detail the life histories of the characters against the background of the social and economic history which they and their kind collectively produce. On the other hand there are the countless tedious passages of seemingly interpolated philosophical and metaphysical discourse which are apparently intended to serve as the vehicle for Mr. Wolfert's idea or theme. Ideally, the material should be impenetrable to analysis of this sort. There should not be two kinds at all, but one. The body of the novel should consist of a single, fully objectified unit of dramatic meaning, complete in itself and demonstrating through its own symbolic and imagistic properties the philosophical implications which are intended to rise out of it. This is the great lesson we have learned in the novel since Flaubert and Henry James. But it is a lesson which Mr. Wolfert's experience and cast of mind do not allow him to learn. His narrative moves along like a vastly independent convoy laden with action, while his philosophy is made to race after it and weave in and out through it like a police patrol heavy with monitory intent. And what is more, the narrative and the philosophy have behind them two completely different and violently incompatible systems of perceiving and explaining the reality which it is the business of the novel to engage.

The narrative is oriented on the old-fashioned historical-naturalist premise, a belief in the efficacy of sheer horizontally accumulated detail to produce a convincing picture of reality. Its traditional literary form is the saga, chronicle, fake journal, and the kind of novel which has come down to us through Zola, Balzac, Norris, Dreiser, and Farrell. Its traditional technique is garrulity. Its traditional goal is not literature but the reproduction of life. Philosophically, it represents a rationale which has been untenable for the last fifty years; for the findings of nineteenth-century European scholarship on which it is based have been that long in the discard. It assumes a mechanical universe governed by natural law and force and a static view of human behavior as simply a chemical and ganglionic response to environmental stimuli; and that is not the universe we have inhabited or a view we have been able sensibly to hold since the appearance of Freud and the publication, in 1905, of the first Einstein papers.

The burden of Mr. Wolfert's philosophy, however, is existentialist, in the respect that it assumes a relative universe and a view of human destiny as an achievement of the responsible or "engaged" will operating within an order of time, space, and nature which is quite the opposite of the mechanical order of the naturalists. Its traditional literary form is the novel of introspection and sensibility, the novel of James, Virginia Woolf, Conrad, and Faulkner, where dramatic realization is as a rule achieved through the realization of a character's power of free choice, his attainment of selfhood.

The question it asks, the question that is asked over and over again in the speculative portions of Mr. Wolfert's novel, is: What can a man do to bring about such a realization in terms of his whole nature? But the question which the narrative asks is: How can a man gain sufficient freedom from the social and economic trap in which environment and chance have placed him to find out whether he has a nature? It is clearly the first of these questions which Mr. Wolfert wishes his novel to answer, or at least to raise; but he has chosen to raise it within the framework of a narrative technique which, by the very nature of the world view it represents, can provide an answer only to the second. The result is that, even as Mr. Wolfert raises his question, his narrative rules it out of order; even as he struggles to save the souls of his characters, his narrative damns them. It is only at the very end of the novel, through what we must interpret as a sacrificial act of self-sabotage, that he is able to impose salvation on them; but by then it is much too late.

The terms in which the characters are introduced to us, the only terms in which, given Mr. Wolfert's method, they can be introduced, are those of naturalist determinism. This is to say that they are seen as the passive victims of forces set in motion by the environment surrounding them—in particular, by the psychological environment created through their relations with their immediate families. In the case of each of the leading characters the directing compulsive force is Oedipal: each in his own way must kill his father in order to release the self-creating principle within himself. This might well have served as the scaffolding on which Mr. Wolfert could have constructed his existentialist novel if he had been able to persuade his narrative to cooperate. But the insight into the psychological nature of his characters which he gives us, largely through his expository passages, is obscured and finally vitiated by the contradictory motives which his narrative causes his characters to have. Wes Olmstead, his prototypal tycoon, is *shown* to be driven, not by an impulse toward creative selfhood, but by an ultimately self-destroying desire for wealth and power; and the vast industrial empire which he builds in the service of this desire comes to represent the ultimate in spiritual impoverishment for the men under him. Elizabeth, his wife, while also ostensibly motivated by a need to become "existent" as a self and as a woman, is *shown* to be motivated by impulses no less acquisitive than her husband's when she undertakes a political career.

It is perhaps because Mr. Wolfert sensed and sought to reverse the direction in which his narrative was taking him that he chose, at the last possible moment, to resolve his characters in terms of an existentialist destiny. Olmstead, at the end of his life and in complete contradiction of the facts of his nature as previously given, is made to develop a conscience and to work for the creative betterment of his men. Elizabeth later on is inexplicably released into womanhood by Olmstead's death and, even more inexplicably, by the suicide of Banty Springer, a former Olmstead employee whom she scarcely knows.

But Mr. Wolfert's last desperate efforts are not entirely wasted. The story of Banty Springer, which forms the long concluding section of the novel, is surely one of the finest pieces of sustained narrative writing to be produced by an American novelist in many years. It is like the scenes of Joe

Christmas's castration in Faulkner's *Light in August* and Axel Heyst's sacrificial death in Conrad's *Victory,* in the sense that it represents one of those rare and almost unbearably lucid moments when all the tensions and ambiguities and, in this case, contradictions which have been spreading through a novel and holding it back from climax suddenly release and resolve themselves in a single tranquillizing act of perfectly rendered drama. But with all its perfection, Banty Springer's story is still not enough to save the novel. The thick tissue of paradox and inconsistency which has grown up before it in the narrative has already crowded out the master design in which it might have taken a significant place.

In these times of indiscriminate praise and blame, one further distinction needs still to be made. *Married Men* may be a crashing bore and a nearly crashing failure. But even at its most boring it is always serious, and even in its failure it testifies in a major way to the high quality of Mr. Wolfert's intent, the continued purity of his aspiration. It also stands well above the majority of the novels which, in its size and form, it so much resembles and with which it is certain to be compared. I mean those voluminous provocations to aphasia which go by the publicity names of "saga" and "chronicle" and "epic" and "panorama" and which seem to prophesy, in their every line, the coming of that day when the publishing of books in America will at last have been delegated to a gigantic autonomous printing machine, whose business it will be to turn out great bundles of paper between gaudy covers, to be sold in the millions to an audience so anesthetized that it will no longer know or care that there is no print whatever on any of the pages.

NINE

The education of James T. Farrell

Reflections at Fifty brought together in 1954 what James T. Farrell considered to be the most interesting of the literary and occasional essays he had written in recent years. It is not an important collection, for Farrell is not an important mind, except by comparison with what in America we deem to be mentality in the creative artist, nor is his influence as a novelist or critic any longer to be very seriously reckoned with. He now has, to be sure, a kind of "place" in American letters; we judge him perhaps as the last of the *natural* writers in the tradition stemming from Norris and Dreiser; and recently he has taken on something of that curiosity or luxury value which writers in this country tend around fifty to come into by virtue of the fact—which we somehow never cease to find remarkable—that like Clark Gable and Gary Cooper they have managed to survive to that age. But one cannot say of

Farrell that he promises to share with us a productive old age in the manner of Shaw or Mann, or that at some time prior to old age we can expect him to resume work upon the foundation which he began to build with *Studs Lonigan* and has since incessantly begun to build over. We therefore find him in this volume engaged upon a typical menopausal literary effort: the consolidation of ideas and insights which he experienced to a greater purpose twenty years ago and which represent a defensive position which is no longer under attack. The book nevertheless is an instructive document, the record of an interesting, serious, and at times almost ludicrously earnest intelligence, and it instructs us best on those occasions when it does not appear to know how much it is instructing us in the way that intelligence educated itself, and in the role which self-education played in shaping the attitudes, morals, and modes to which that intelligence gave expression in literature.

Self-education comes high in America, and Farrell has paid for it—as in differing respects have Faulkner and Hemingway—with his whole career. Its cost to him consists in the fact that the attitudes it has given him are largely provincial; the morals are parochial; and the modes are pedantic, for it appears to be the case with the self-educated literary man in America that he tends always to confuse learning and pedantry and that in pursuing the one he will caricature the other. This, I take it, was part of Henry James's point about Hawthorne. But for an intelligence of a different quality and grain from Farrell's the cost is not necessarily so high. The self-educated critic R. P. Blackmur, for example, is similarly afflicted with pedantry; in some areas he has informed himself to a degree that is very nearly saintly. But Blackmur's intelligence derives its great compulsive force from precisely its ignorance of what the formal limits and conventions of learning are, of just how much work it has to do in order to graduate at the head of its class. The result is that in the course of expiating his ignorance (which I am certain he always believes to be profound) Blackmur outmodes the conventions by exceeding them. His fear of flunking out flunks out nine-tenths of his contemporaries. Farrell's pedantry, on the other hand, is of a peculiarly low order and flaccid kind, the kind that caricatures itself because it is backed by a knowledge of what the conventions are and how to imitate them.

It becomes clear in reading over the prose in this volume that Farrell went to school, but it is just as clear that he went to school to the wrong teachers. His prose is a savage compound of jargon and rhetoric derived from French naturalist novels, the writings of William James, John Dewey, the Marxists, and the German philosophers, political manifestoes, and behaviorist psychology, and it appears to have got into the book by way of the dump truck and shovel. It has no rhythm, grace, warmth, or subtlety of style, and it is overlaid with a heavy-footed earnestness and zeal like that of a frightened schoolboy, pompous and popeyed, reciting a speech cribbed largely from the *Encyclopædia Britannica*. In content it is approximately vintage 1910. I do not mean that the questions it raises are necessarily no longer in force. It is rather that one no longer expects to see them discussed in quite this fashion and at this level. It is scarcely real any longer, for example, to observe of naturalism, as Farrell observes of it in one of these essays, that "it has been an attempt to meet and to reveal and to explore the nature of experience in the modern world." We now know that this is exactly what naturalism has consistently failed to do for the modern world and that that is the reason the best modern writers can no longer take it seriously. If they did, they would have to take seriously Newton on the nature of space and Spengler on the nature of Western society. But this is the nature of Farrell's provincialism, one consequence of his self-education, and we have no choice but to take it seriously.

The other consequence, his moral parochialism, is the quality which above all others has impoverished his imagination and concerning the nature of which, by word, tone, and unwitting confession, *Reflections at Fifty* is at times almost heartbreakingly informative. The more purely literary phase of his education Farrell apparently got from two men, Sherwood Anderson and Theodore Dreiser, about both of whom he has written here with honest admiration and feeling. What they passed on to him by precept and example was the great cranky lesson which had sustained them in their own mountainous dedication to their craft: the serious writer in America is a man besieged; lying in wait on all sides of him are forces of darkness and bigotry bent on stealing his virtue; he is a perpetual Penelope and at the same time he must serve as his own avenging Odysseus; his role must be one of unremitting, nerve-end vigilance. Anderson and Dreiser had early developed a paranoid revulsion to being touched; the cry of "Rape!" was forever on their lips; and if they wore their integrity a bit too enticingly high at the knee, it was because their right to integrity, their right to keep it or give it away, was constantly being challenged. And this was the crux of Farrell's education in literary morals. Anderson and Dreiser taught him integrity; they took him aside and patted him on the head and told him always to speak the truth, my son, and no harm will ever come to you. They helped to develop in him the one quality for which today we rightly do him honor.

But then Farrell stopped learning. He stopped right then and there with what he had and set himself up in practice as a writer of novels, a man of integrity, a speaker of the truth, all of which he was. The one truth he had was the truth of his early life on the south side of Chicago when he was Studs Lonigan–cum–Danny O'Neill–cum–James T. Farrell, and after the manner of an Anderson "grotesque," he made this one truth his own. Then he began to discover that, just as his teachers had warned, there were dark forces about striving to keep him from speaking the truth. There were court injunctions, hostile critics, leagues of frightened philistines. His integrity was being threatened, and all that he knew to do, all that his education had taught him to do, was to speak the truth again and again in novel after novel until the dark forces either surrendered or were destroyed. It did not matter that it was substantially the same truth he spoke each time. The important thing was that it was The Truth. He began to develop a compulsion, a repetition compulsion. Finally it became a fixture of his psychic life. He would sit in the midst of his own entrails, weaving them all day into a tapestry which he would unweave all night, just to keep the dark forces off guard. But he never learned how to be his own Odysseus. Even in middle age, while flying in a plane from Los Angeles to New York or while talking with a Russian official in Vienna, he tells us that his mind was not there, was not absorbing and recording fresh experience; it was back in the childhood world of his first and only truth with "Old Tom and Mary O'Flaherty, Jim and Liz O'Neill, Aunt Margaret, Aunt Louise, Uncle Al, little Danny." The integrity that became an obsession, the integrity that made him an honest writer, has held fast to the truth, and the truth now holds Farrell fast, blocking his ascent into the greatness that might have been his. It has forced him instead deeper and deeper into his pedantry, his thick, almost scholastic preoccupation with every last physical detail of his world, until in his last novel *The Face of Time* we find even the details running out and the truth narrowing to the little circle of infancy and age. And above the monotonous drone of the language, doing its remorseless work of genealogy tracing and visceral bookkeeping, we catch the accents of a man nearly catatonic, telling over the catechism which he was taught would eventually get him to Heaven.

TEN

The function of the book critic

THIS IS TO ASSUME that the "book" critic, as distinct from the formal literary critic and the historian of ideas, may be said still to have a function, and I am by no means sure we are safe in assuming this. Certainly his function, if he has one, is not what it was in that distant and now somewhat overly memorialized day when, as Lionel Trilling remarked, "criticism existed in heroic practical simplicity, when it was all truth against hypocrisy, idealism against philistinism, and the opposite of 'romanticism' was not 'classicism' but 'realism,' which—it now seems odd—negated both." We no longer feel ourselves at home with such ideas, nor do our serious critics, the best of whom, by a fine irony, have been the ones responsible for depriving criticism—hence themselves—of those convenient verbal oppositions in terms of which its heroism was formerly defined. We conceive of criticism far more snobbishly now; we know, we take pleasure in knowing that it is no longer heroic, practical, or simple, but is at least an institution or a mining operation if not the whole of literature itself.

Still, for the purposes of searching out a function for the "book" critic, the older, humbler conception should serve us best, even though we should be hard pressed to find anyone today able or willing to work within it; for a principal motive behind the search is to insist upon a recovery of some of the force of the older conception, the salvage of a little of the heroism, practicality, and simplicity. I assume it as axiomatic that criticism is capable of infinite extension beyond the carefully patrolled borders now set up for it, and that this extension should commence with the restoration to full usefulness of the critic whose business was once the disinterested discussion of books, past and present, within the matrix of taste and close judgment.

This is not to suggest that we substitute one mining operation for another. If it were, we should soon have to recognize that we were having to market a very poor ore indeed and be quickly out of business. But it is to suggest that we mine for a better ore in the same general area, keeping before us always the fact that what we are looking for must measure up to the change which has rendered conditions far different from what they were when we mined there in the past. This change consists not merely of technological advance; it involves a full-scale reorientation of the relationship which once obtained between literature and the public imagination, between the written word, the literary image, and the power of that imagination to dramatize itself, to find extensions and confirmations of itself, in words and images, the humanizing faculty of language.

I take it for granted that the integrity of this relationship has today very nearly broken down and that it was beginning to break down even in the age of critical heroism and simplicity. That is what gave criticism then its special urgency and force: its insistence upon bringing and holding together the strands of language and a public imagination which was no longer quite at ease with, or convinced of the necessity of, the union. But there nonetheless still existed in that age a sense of the reality of both language and literature in an audience of what Henry Ladd Smith once called "the superior few," and it was to this audience that the older type of book critic addressed himself. He wrote his reviews and essays for such journals of liberal opinion as the *New Republic* and *Nation;* he discussed books and ideas in a literate, intelligent fashion, and the "few" understood and responded, oftentimes vehemently, oftentimes boorishly, but they responded, because they too read and at their leisure discussed books and ideas in a cultural atmosphere, however thinning, in which both had a living relation to the daily conduct of life.

If we say that in recent years that relation has become increasingly tenuous or severed, we have to take into account the shift that has occurred in the public's position with regard to all works of serious art as well as the anesthetizing effects of mass education and the mass media, and we have to keep in mind also that it is not only to art that the public no longer fully responds but to most of the art substitutes which we like to hold accountable for the failure of responsiveness to art. Radio, the motion pictures, and television have all begun to suffer the same fate, which is to be subjected to a decline of public interest even as the mass of the public gives to them daily more and more of its time and concentration.

The shift I speak of issues at least partly from a dwindling of the public capacity for sustained attention in all areas, and this has something to do both with the atomization of the individual self under the stresses of modern life and with the retreat of the mass psyche from circumstances which threaten to overpower and "flood" it with more stimuli than it can safely absorb. The human mind, to paraphrase Eliot, cannot bear too much reality, and when it is asked to—which is the hourly request of our time—it does not automatically fall back into that fantasy state in which literature takes on its strongest appeal as a device for channeling and discharging the unwanted sensations. It is far more likely to sink instead into a slough of protective detachment and ennui from which neither literature nor any palliative substitute can be counted on to arouse it. Literature for the mass mind then becomes—if it becomes at all—a thing which one merely consumes like Seltzer in an unceasing, fretful search for relief from one's sense of inner disquietude, and not only is its original integrity as a humanizing organism destroyed in the process, but its basic nature is gradually altered until finally it is smoothed and pasteurized into simply another of the divertive products of a culture bent on entertaining itself to death.

The automation both of the materials and the capacities of mass response has caused the whole of our cultural potential to become polarized at the extremes of special cultural interest. The best and most serious elements are now centralized in the universities (an inevitable but dangerous development), the worst and most fraudulent in the market place of popular entertainment. The solid middle formerly provided by the "superior few" has fallen away, scattering the few among the many between and at the extremes, and depriving the intellectual world of a liaison point between the areas of practical affairs and ideas. As this has occurred, the standards furnished out of the older humanistic education of the few have become hallucinated and bowdlerized in a frenzy of commercialized effort to pander to the tastes and appearances of taste created by the diffusion of interests and appropriated by the new semiliterate mass. That portion of the mass, for example, which has acquired or likes to fancy it has acquired a taste for books is given the illusion of absorbing and advancing the "modern" through the attention regularly given in the fashion magazines to the décor literature of certain younger writers. That this "modern" had already become a cliché before it had had time to become serious is a fact of no concern to a public so sophisticated that it accepts—in company with half the visiting insurance salesmen from Seattle—the antiquated plays of Tennessee Williams as if they were in the very forefront of dramatic experimentalism, antiquated in the sense that they are concocted out of the scrap-basket materials of the naturalistic theater of the thirties and are merely the Broadway analogue of the sex-crime-and-violence films which the lower orders of the same public twitch and shudder at in the theaters across the street.

But the automation of mass response has had its most devastating effects upon the processes of cultural production itself. The products for which the educated tastes of the few formerly created a demand and which the continuous exercise of those tastes sustained at a high level of quality have now become promiscuously available on the mass market, and that portion of the public to whom all tastes are foreign has grown content to accept the advice of the market on nearly all matters relating to consumption. This is to say that the market has taken over from the public the primary and crucial act of taste along with the act of setting the standard of quality at which taste shall be considered satisfied. While in a society like ours this kind of paternalism may be educative, as it undoubtedly is in such areas as the cheap production of reprint literature, it has tended to breed a complacency and passivity, a spurious sense of things arranged and under control, both in the public mind and in the minds of those whose job is the custodianship of taste, the preservation of cultural morals. It is remarkably easy, for example, to conclude from the current proliferation of reprinted classics that ours is indeed an Augustan age, that literature is something signed, officially sealed, and delivered to us by the past, and that as long as we remember to take it out for dusting now and then, we are free to devote ourselves to humbler, less stringent concerns. The publishers perhaps unconsciously enforce this impression, for in the face of a compliant mass market and the prevailing confusion of standards, they often yield to the temptation simply to keep the industry going by publishing whatever the traffic will bear, regardless of whether their consciences will bear it or not. The reviewers, in turn, who would ordinarily be able and willing to separate out the good from the bad, are obliged—since they have nothing else—to accept what the publishers place on the market, and because they too must work to keep the industry going, they tend to treat the good and the bad with an indiscriminate seriousness, hence, with an indiscriminate perfunctoriness, with the result that the good and the bad stand about an equal chance of success and failure. The reviewer's life quite literally depends upon this kind of compromise, for with countless numbers of mediocre books at his disposal, he is forced either to treat them seriously or to deny that he has any justification for treating them at all. What usually happens is that the conscientious reviewer will give himself the illusion of integrity by singling out for overpraise some book which *looks* serious or which, at any rate, contains elements he remembers as having been identified with the seriousness of certain books of the past, however dull and stereotyped they may have since become. It is very nearly endemic to present-day reviewers that in the absence of a renewing standard of critical values they will eulogize the conventional and condemn the original. The conventional they see as original, while the original appears to them artificial or bizarre or phony. But the precision of the reviewers' judgments is no longer a matter of very grave concern, for the idea is, as I have suggested, quite soundly established in the public mind that literature is a task completed, its issues settled with a finality which renders the reviewers' judgments academic, and that if one should ever have occasion to refer to it, one should look not to current productions but to the classics or, better still, to that sacred bibliographical fount from which all good pocket-sized books spring, the fabulous 1920s.

This attitude is yet another result of the breakdown of the public capacity for response to language, and it has undoubtedly had more to do than any other factor with the change which has occurred in the American literary situation. We look back today as upon some remote geological era to the time not so very long ago when books were able to touch and hold the imagination of the reading public, the great time of furor and controversy centering in such works as *All the King's Men, Raintree County,* and *Under the Volcano.* These are all novels of the 1940s, and it is perfectly true that since then the culture has entered on a period of consolidation and stasis characterized by the absence of those large, motivating ideas which usually serve in fiction to provide a link between the world of public affairs and the world of artifice.

But it is equally true that the 1940s represented the opening phase of the polarization of our cultural interests, the scattering of the "superior few," and the beginning of the recession of the public imagination from the symbolic arena of language. Both in those years and in the decades immediately preceding them literature stood in a much closer relation to immediate experience than it does today, and the agencies whose function it is to hold the life of literature in trust were still engaged —albeit with increasing desperateness—in monitoring the public taste. It is a fact of wonderment now that a critic of the stature of Edmund Wilson could succeed through the 1940s in influencing large sectors of that taste with a criticism both learned and urbane. But we should not forget that at the same time almost the whole of our literary intellectual class was still concerned with contemporary literature and was not above commenting upon it. The book sections of the *New Republic, The Nation,* and *The New Yorker* up to roughly the end of World War II constitute a record of the kind of communication that was once possible between serious criticism and the remnants of the literate public.

But the literary intellectual class today is centered for the most part in the small academic quarterlies; the serious critics are represented in their pages by essays on Dante and Melville; and what little time they devote to contemporary literature is usually given over to the writing of "Fiction Chronicles," package review-essays in which six or eight new novels are treated with a cold detachment befitting the low opinion in which new work generally is held. The counterpart of Edmund Wilson, should he appear today, would soon have the sense of shouting into a bottomless pit, for if a literate public still exists for the *New Republic, The Nation,* and *The New Yorker,* its members have grown apathetic to literary questions or too busy with their own affairs to respond to them.

As for the counterparts of the serious novels of the past, it is perhaps only emptily brash in these times to observe that we have had several, of which two of the most recent are, to my mind, William Gaddis's *The Recognitions* and Alan Harrington's *The Revelations of Doctor Modesto.* Both of these novels possess merits and idiosyncrasies remarkable enough to have aroused a storm of critical controversy and to have won them a fair public following had they been published ten or fifteen years ago, when an Edmund Wilson might have performed for them the service he performed for the younger Hemingway or a Malcolm Cowley for the neglected older Faulkner. Instead, they were allowed to pass from publication into oblivion with nothing in between to arrest their passage. *The Recognitions* received indifferent to stupid notice in the leading New York literary supplements, and *The Revelations of Doctor Modesto,* in keeping with the policy currently governing the review of serious first novels, was accorded brief and insipid notice in the very back pages of *The New York Times Book Review*. One explanation may be that both books, like all serious novels, present an imaginative view of the truly contemporary world, while the mass of the public and most of the reviewers have never grown beyond the view which was fashionable in the 1920s. But whatever the reason, it is difficult to understand how the reward of reputation can ever come to the author of either novel, for there exists at present no agency able or willing to keep their names alive in the public consciousness until the time when they publish their next books. There is no assurance, furthermore, that when that time comes they will fare any differently, except that the chances are excellent they will run afoul of the prevailing hostility to second novels and be obliterated once and for all. Without at least a small receptive audience and a body of critical opinion capable of accepting the risks of its obligation to new literature, the publication of books must become for these writers what Allen Tate called "a series of pragmatic conquests which . . . are true only in some other world than that inhabited by men," or a nightmare experience such as Scott Fitzgerald described of "standing at twilight on a deserted range, with an empty rifle in my hands and the targets down. No problem set—simply a silence with only the sound of my own breathing."

It is evident, then, that at the moment we should be hard pressed to find a book critic upon whom to bestow the accolade of "function." Where in the present circumstances of society would he discharge a "function" if he had it? The older type of book critic has almost entirely disappeared with the shift of literary power from the open frontier of the "superior few" to the closed circle of the university; many writers who began their careers as book critics are now university critics performing in the quarterlies an altogether different function. In the market place we have many reviewers but no critic with an authoritative voice whose daily or weekly business is the close supervision and enrichment of taste. Our reviewers are free-lance writers, hack writers, professors who write, literary journalists, but not men of letters. They are neither committed with their whole minds to literary values nor educated in the history of literary ideas and movements. Their treatment of books is consequently superficial, arbitrary, and undisciplined. The serious weekly periodicals are no longer outlets for informed literary discussion; their book sections differ scarcely at all from those of the newspapers. The book critic with a desire to form himself in the older tradition is faced, therefore, with a choice between occasional reviewing and even more occasional quarterly publication, but if he wishes to concern himself frequently and at length with contemporary work, to discharge in full his responsibilities to new writers and reputations, neither will afford him the space he needs.

His only hope, and it is at best a scant one, is that out of the present cultural ferment will emerge a new audience composed, perhaps, of the younger people who are obliged today to bear in silence their disaffection with the state of literary affairs but who will one day be able to assert themselves. In the meantime, he will probably be forced to work in isolation and obscurity. If he goes under, he will at least have the satisfaction of knowing that the culture that bred him and gave him his function has gone under too, that the silence is at last complete, the targets are down for good.

INDEX

ABOUT THE AUTHOR

John W. Aldridge was born in Sioux City, Iowa, in 1922 but at an early age migrated with his parents to Tennessee and settled on a small farm. In 1940 he entered the University of Chattanooga as a county scholarship student, shortly became editor of the campus newspaper, and in 1942 was awarded a fellowship for study at the Bread Loaf School of English. Mr. Aldridge entered the Army in 1943 and served through the war with the XX Corps in Europe. Following his discharge he resumed his university studies at the University of California at Berkeley, where he became editor of *Occident*. He was graduated in 1947, and later in the same year he published in *Harper's Magazine* a controversial article on the new postwar generation of American writers. In 1948, Mr. Aldridge was appointed Lecturer in criticism and in 1950 assistant professor of English at the University of Vermont. In 1948–1950, he organized and directed at Vermont a yearly symposium on the current American novel, and in 1951–1953 he established the School of Modern Critical Studies, in which Allen Tate, R. P. Blackmur, David Daiches, and other writers and critics participated. In the summers of 1952 and 1953 he served also as director of the Fiction Writers Conference held at Putney, Vermont, and in 1953 he founded and edited with the novelist Vance Bourjaily the literary magazine *Discovery*. In 1953 Mr. Aldridge participated as a lecturer, along with Hannah Arendt, V. S. Pritchett, and Sean O'Faolain, in the Christian Gauss Seminars in Criticism at Princeton University. It was at Princeton that he completed work on the basic material for *In Search of Heresy*.

Mr. Aldridge's first critical book *After the Lost Generation* was published by McGraw-Hill in 1951. A year later Ronald Press issued a college textbook of criticism compiled under his editorship, *Critiques and Essays on Modern Fiction*. Since 1949, he has been a frequent contributor of reviews and essays to the

Saturday Review, The New York Times Book Review, Partisan Review, Western Review, Virginia Quarterly Review, and *New Republic,* and in 1955 *The Nation* announced him as a regular contributor. Mr. Aldridge has lectured in universities throughout the country, including Boston University, City College of New York, Columbia, Princeton, University of Wyoming, Oberlin, and Skidmore. He has done research in literary scholarship for the Rockefeller Foundation, and is spending the current year traveling and writing in Europe.